WHO

IS

KEMEKA

BENJAMIN?

The half hasn't been told but, as you delve between the pages of this book; you will discover who the world says that Kemeka is and who God says that she is.

Kemeka Benjamin-Williams

1

COPYRIGHT

DEDICATION

I dedicate this book to all individuals who have experienced sexual or spiritual abuse, and those who carry emotional wounds.

It's for anyone who has felt unloved, rejected, or burdened by shame due to past or present mistakes.

It's for those who face mental challenges daily, striving for acceptance.

To anyone grappling with their identity in God and seeking guidance on how to live for Him. And to those who have turned away from God, struggling to find their way back.

ACKNOWLEDGEMENTS

I extend my gratitude to the Holy Spirit of God, my source of comfort and wisdom.

I'm deeply thankful for my mother, Evangelist Annette Williams-Grant, a steadfast prayer warrior who continuously interceded for my protection, health, and purpose in serving God. Her unwavering love remained steadfast, even upon learning of the challenges and traumas I faced.

I'm indebted to my hardworking father, Clinton Benjamin, whose tireless efforts, especially during harsh winter seasons in America, paved the way for my migration, enabling me to start afresh and evolve into the woman I am today.

To my husband Pastor Kelly Williams, brother Sheldon Fuller, sisters Evangelist Sashikia Benjamin and Evangelist Shelly- Ann Lamont who listen to my testimonies, uplift and support me. Your attentive ears and unwavering support have been invaluable.

I am profoundly grateful for the divine helpers and obedient leaders sent by the Holy Spirit, who accompanied me from childhood to adulthood, offering guidance and support through my trials and tribulations.

To all those who lifted me in prayer as guided by the Holy Spirit, petitioning for my safety, ministry, and overall well-being, I offer my heartfelt thanks.

Even to those who opposed me, their challenges served as catalysts for seeking refuge and finding peace in God, ultimately strengthening my faith.

Special appreciation goes to my publisher for their role in bringing this work to fruition.

TABLE OF CONTENTS

Chapter #:	Title	Page #

Table of contents (Cont'd)

Table of contents (Cont'd)

INTRODUCTION

Join me on a journey through my life, a journey that led me to question why bad things seemed to happen to me, why even those who claimed to love me sometimes treated me poorly.

I grappled with my anger towards God for seemingly not answering my prayers and for the challenges I faced.

But as you continue reading, you'll discover how my perspective shifted. I began to see things through the lens of God's plan for my life, and I started following His guidance.

This transformation allowed me to become the person I am today: free, healed, delivered, and filled with love, all through the grace of God.

This is the story of my spiritual journey, a journey

filled with challenges, revelations, and ultimately, redemption.

WHO WAS KEMEKA?

On the Surface I was smiling but inside; I was crumbling.

I found myself in a state of deep confusion, frustration, and depression. I was enduring abuse, and my mind was clouded with thoughts and voices that left me feeling isolated and judged by others.

On the surface, I wore a smile and shared laughter, but inside, I was crumbling, yearning for an escape to heaven to be with my Heavenly Father, Jehovah.

In my despair, I became increasingly selfish, failing to consider the impact my actions had on my Creator and those who loved me. It was as if my world revolved solely around my suffering and the longing to be my authentic self, to experience love on my own terms, with all my wants and needs.

Amid the chaos of my thoughts, there was a soothing, reassuring voice that often guided me, offering wisdom and caution.

I didn't always comprehend why I had knowledge of certain things before they occurred, nor did I recognize that it was the Holy Spirit speaking to me. He was a constant presence, trying to help me, but I frequently ignored His guidance.

Chapter One

CHILDHOOD LIFE STORY

"I praise you because I am fearfully and wonderfully made; your works are wonderful; I know that full well." Psalm 139:14 (NIV):

In my early years:

As a baby, I was absolutely adorable with chubby cheeks that everyone couldn't resist pinching. However, I had an aversion to people touching my face, and this discomfort continued as I grew up. I often found myself telling people not to put their hands on my face, as I associated it with having dirty hands that might cause breakouts.

Have you ever experienced something similar?

I was fortunate to grow up in a loving and caring family. My parents, Annette and Clinton, were there for me, providing the support and love I needed. In their presence, I always felt wanted and cherished.

I can relate to the experience of living in a one-bedroom space with everyone in the family until we were able to upgrade to a two-bedroom living arrangement. Those were humble beginnings.

Let me share a story about my first pet, a beautiful rooster with a multitude of colors.

I adored that rooster, but one day, I heard that someone in the neighborhood was stealing people's chickens. I had no safe place to hide my beloved rooster, and sadly, the next morning, he was gone. I was heartbroken, and at that moment, I vowed never to get another pet.

In my adult life

However, as an adult, I decided to welcome two turtles into my life. They reminded me of how life can sometimes move at a slow pace, but they also symbolized resilience and never giving up.

I have fond memories of attending church with my mom. Even if she couldn't go, she would make sure my brother, sister, and I attended. Sunday school was a favorite part of the experience.

I enjoyed the games, and most of all, I loved learning about God.

One time in Sunday school, we played a scavenger hunt, and I found a special gift, which made me really happy. Christmas time was a highlight for me because I got to sing and act in the Christmas play. Acting was so much fun, and pretending to be changed by God from a sinner to someone who doesn't sin anymore was a great experience.

I remember one particular song we sang during these events, "Go Tell It on the Mountain." The lyrics went, "Once I was a smoker, I used to smoke both day and night, but Jesus saw me smoking and he took me by my hand and said, 'Go tell it on the mountain, over the hills and everywhere, go tell it on the mountain that Jesus Christ was born.'"

I always looked forward to special events at church because it meant I could perform and be a part of something truly special.

Time to Change

As I grew older and heard the stories of how Jesus Christ died on the cross for my sins, it deeply moved me. I couldn't help but feel the pain He endured from the beatings He received. One Sunday, the burden became too much to bear, and I knew I had to make a change.

I told my Sunday School teacher that I wanted to get baptized because I couldn't go on without giving my life to Jesus, who had given His life for me.

The next Sunday, it was announced at church that I would be baptized, along with several other children. My grandmother on my father's side was overjoyed, but my mother was initially skeptical, thinking I might be joking because it was so sudden.

She didn't attend this baptism but the second baptism in 2012. However, that night of my first baptism, I felt a deep sense of peace and fulfillment as I gave my life to Jehovah and washed away my sins through baptism.

I was spirited and feisty.

I was a spirited and feisty little girl, and I knew how to use some choice words. The day after my baptism, I got angry at someone at school and let out a few curse words.

To my surprise, someone who knew I had been baptized the night before confronted me, asking, "Didn't you get baptized last night?"

I sheepishly replied, "Yes." It was my first slip, but I was just a child, and I forgot that I shouldn't be using such language. I did try my best to be good and do right.

I have fond memories of my dad. I'd often share secrets and whispers with him, so no one else could hear. He would put me on his shoulders and play with me, which I loved. Spending time with my dad was wonderful.

He had left Jamaica for America to work and provide for me, my sisters, and my brothers. He was very protective of me, and I proudly admit that I was his favorite.

As for my mother, Annette, she was incredibly sweet and caring. I would confide in her about everything, even the not- so-good things in my life. Even though I was living with my father's parents, my mother still took great care of me.

My mother did so much for me. She would wash my clothes, comb my hair for school, attend parent-teacher meetings, have church suits tailored for me, and so many other things.

I felt a deep connection with my sister Curly, I thought we may be twins because we sometimes wore the same colors and designs, and we were both born in July. Even though I didn't live with my mother, she still did everything a mother should do.

I was competitive

During my time in basic school, I was a smart student, and there was one classmate who was equally bright. We had a friendly competition going on between us.

As I moved on to primary school, I continued to perform well academically but had a penchant for getting into fights. I was fiercely protective and wouldn't allow anyone to harm me or the people I cared about. I was a defender of what I believed to be right, and I stood up for my sisters and cousins.

After lunch, the principal would often call out the names of students who had caused trouble during lunchtime, and my name was frequently on that list. Those of us on the list would receive punishment, including a beating and sometimes being made to sit

16

in a bookroom for a while.

One day, I witnessed something unpleasant happening behind the lantern and decided to walk away. To my surprise, my name wasn't called that afternoon, and I felt relieved.

My grandmother owned a shop in our community, and sometimes she would give me candy to sell at school. I enjoyed selling them, and the other kids loved the candies.

On Fridays, I would wear pretty dresses to school. However, some of the teachers didn't seem to like me, possibly due to my family background. Despite that, I took pride in myself and my achievements.

My mother was my advocate

I had a fourth-grade teacher who I felt didn't like me, and I couldn't understand why because I was never rude to her. Her expressions toward me were often unpleasant.

One day, a male student punched me, and I promptly left the classroom.

I walked about 2 miles or more back home to tell my mother about it. She then took me back to school and informed the teacher of what had happened.

The teacher was quite surprised, and I boldly told her that I had gotten my mother because I felt she didn't like me. That evening, I stood up to the boy who had punched me, and he never touched me again.

It's remarkable that despite this teacher not liking me, I was determined to excel in my studies. I achieved high grades on my exams, and my performance was so good that they allowed me to skip grade five and move directly to grade six.

I still remember the day she called my name with a smile, and I was thrilled because I felt like I had proven that I wasn't a loser.

Another moment when she showed happiness for me was when I successfully passed my Common Entrance Exams. I was genuinely surprised when she congratulated me.

Sixth grade posed quite a challenge during my primary school days.

I had a strict teacher who appeared to single me out, and on top of that, I was grappling with issues both at home and in school.

Despite my commendable performance, this teacher didn't consistently acknowledge it with the stars I deserved.

My mother had to step in, speaking to the teacher and advocating for my rights. I'm incredibly thankful for my mom, who became my defender, fighting on my behalf.

Recognizing my struggles with memory, she even went the extra mile, investing in extra lessons to ensure I was well- prepared for my classes and upcoming Common Entrance Exams.

Words and numbers presented quite a challenge for me. I frequently confused the meanings of words, and there was a particular incident during a synonym test where nervousness led me to give a completely different answer, resulting in failure.

Being put on the spot and grappling with numbers posed difficulties for me. Additionally, I had a tendency to read things backward. It wasn't until adulthood that I came to the realization that I had dyslexia.

It's truly remarkable that my mom's assistance with homework and the invaluable extra lessons played a pivotal role in my success.

Achieving high grades in my Common Entrance Exams was a significant accomplishment, and the cherry on top was securing a spot in the top class at Seaforth High School, specifically 7'one.

My mother's support and the extra lessons played a crucial role in my success.

Passing my Common Entrance Exams with high grades is a significant achievement and making it into the top class at Seaforth High School must was a proud moment for myself and my mother.

Revisiting Experiences

Let me revisit some of the experiences I had in school.

I had a strong aversion to bullies, and I would stand up to anyone who tried to fight me. I never backed down and often tried to protect my sisters and friends from bullies.

However, at home, my grandmother would sometimes punish me for things my cousins did or for very minor reasons. I received so many beatings that I stopped crying and would just stand there enduring the punishment.

When she noticed that I wasn't crying anymore, she would say, "You're not crying, child," and then she would hit me even more and harder, and I would start crying because I wanted her to stop.

I became so angry that I would sometimes pout and make my face look ugly. I would also curse in my head. I learned bad words from hearing my neighbors use them. Despite the times when she was kind to me, I could tell that there was an influence on her behavior that made her treat me poorly.

Playing Grown up

I noticed something strange when older men would look at me and smile. I would smile back and be polite, but none of them ever touched me inappropriately.

I liked boys at school, and they liked me too. It was all very innocent since we were just kids. We played games where we pretended to be husband and wife or acted like children.

We would sit beside each other in class and sometimes walk home together.

<u>Reflect on your childhood and remember if you made bad covenants that need to be broken, break them now in the name of Jesus Christ.</u>

During a recent vacation to Jamaica, I saw orange grass called "love grass," and it reminded me of my childhood. We used to pick that grass, roll it up, spit on it, and then throw it back into the bushes, declaring that we would always love each other.

We would check every time we passed by to see if the love grass had grown. However, the Lord revealed to me that I needed to break the covenant I had made with my primary school boyfriend.

We were young and didn't understand the significance of what we were doing by making such a covenant. So, I prayed right then and there, breaking that covenant.

Home wasn't a place for Games.

Home wasn't the place for games due to my strict grandmother. Playing opportunities were rare, but when they arose, I relished games like the stone-throwing game, where the goal was to hit someone else's stone.

Marble games, typically dominated by boys, also caught my interest. Additionally, I found success in the rubber bands game, winning a few rounds when playing with other kids who gathered at the shop.

Crafting toy trucks from juice boxes was a source of joy for me. During lonely moments, I'd gather hibiscus leaves, placing them in water and then squeezing them until I extracted oil. There was something special about the process—it felt like I was personally creating my own oil.

Learning the art of cooking from my mother and grandmother turned me into quite a skilled chef. Surprisingly, by the age of 12, I had already mastered the skill of baking.

My grandmother even granted me the opportunity to sell the bake food such a Totto that I bake in her shop and assisted her in selling other food supplies.

It's fantastic that my mother passed down cooking skills to me, and I believed that I picked them up quite well. Becoming adept at baking by the age of 12 was quite an accomplishment! One day my sister Curly and I mix clear clay with sugar and bake it on a wood fire to see how it taste. It came out nice and sweet.

Chapter One

Lessons

'Children and Parent Relationships'

*"Children, obey your parents in the Lord, for this is right. 'Honor your father and mother'—which is the first commandment with a promise—'so that it may go well with you and that you may enjoy long life on the earth.' Fathers, do not exasperate your children; instead, bring them up in the training and instruction of the Lord." (*Ephesians 6:1-4 NIV*)*

Please allow the following lessons to provide a biblical foundation for understanding and fostering healthy relationships between parents, teachers and children, encouraging practical application of these principles in daily life.

CHILDREN

"Children, obey your parents in everything, for this pleases the Lord" (Colossians 3:20 NIV):

- Don't blame your parents for not teaching you something, especially if they were never taught those things themselves.

- Don't blame your parents for not demonstrating love towards you, especially if they themselves were never taught what love truly meant or how to express it.

- Don't blame your parents for leaving you with someone

so that they could go to work to make life better for you.

- Don't hold your parents accountable for entrusting your care to someone else when they were unable to provide for you and seek what they believed was best for your well-being.

- Consider extending forgiveness to your parents and sharing your emotions regarding their departure.

- Hold yourself in high regard and extend respect to both your teachers and classmates.

- Practice kindness and care towards both yourself and others.

- Feel empowered to communicate with your teacher if you believe you're being treated unfairly.

- Feel confident in expressing yourself to your teacher when you don't comprehend a lesson and choose to do so in a private setting.

It's crucial not to hesitate in informing your teacher if you're experiencing bullying or sexual assault. Your safety and well-being are of the utmost importance.

"These commandments that I give you today are to be on your hearts. Impress them on your children. Talk about them when you sit at home and when you walk along the road, when you lie down and when you get up." (Deuteronomy 6:6-7 NIV)

PARENTS

- Parents always spend time talking and listening to your children.

- Parents fight for your child/children rights when your child is right.

- Parents help your child/children with their schoolwork and pay for tutoring if you can.

- Parents believe in your child or children and show it.

- Parents get assistance for your child if he or her has a learning disability.

- Parents learn how love to your child/ children.

- Parents take time to teach your child/children what are classified as bad or good things.

TEACHERS

"Instruct the wise and they will be wiser still; teach the righteous and they will add to their learning." (Proverbs 9:9 NIV)

- Be kind and caring to all children.

- Let the children feel free to come and tell you a problem.

- All children are special.

- Show respect and teach children how to have respect for themselves and others.

- Find time to help children with learning disabilities.

Chapter One

Prayer for Children, Parents and Teacher relationships

Heavenly Father, we come before you with grateful hearts, acknowledging that every good and perfect gift comes from You. Today, we lift up the relationships between children, parents, and teachers into Your loving care.

Prayer For Children

Lord, watch over the children in our families and communities. Guide them in wisdom, love, and understanding. Grant them the strength to navigate the challenges they face and the courage to stand firm in their faith.

Help them to honor their parents and teachers, to be receptive to guidance, and to grow into the individuals You have destined them to be.

Prayer For Parents

Father, bless the parents entrusted with the care and upbringing of these precious children. Grant them patience, wisdom, and discernment. May their homes be filled with love, understanding, and laughter. Strengthen the bonds between parents and children, fostering an environment where Your values are embraced, and Your grace is evident.

Prayer For Teachers

Lord, we lift up the teachers who play a vital role in shaping the minds and hearts of the next generation. Grant them passion for their calling, patience in their challenges, and creativity in their teaching. May they be beacons of knowledge and virtue, imparting not only academic lessons but also life lessons that reflect Your truth.

Prayer For Relationships

Heavenly Father, bind these families and communities together in love. May the relationships between children, parents, and teachers be characterized by mutual respect, open communication, and genuine care for one another. Let Your grace abounds in these interactions, fostering an atmosphere of growth, encouragement, and support.

Prayer For Unity

Lord, we pray for unity among parents and teachers, recognizing the shared responsibility in nurturing the next generation. May they work hand in hand, valuing each other's insights and contributions, for the well-being of the children they serve.

Closing Prayer

Almighty God, we commit these relationships into Your hands. Be the foundation of our families and communities, guiding us with Your wisdom and grace. May the love that flows from Your heart permeate every interaction, creating bonds that withstand the tests of time. In the name of Jesus, we pray. Amen.

Chapter One

- I forgive my parents, grandmother and family members who have hurt me, in the name of Jesus.

- I release myself from the pain caused by my family to me in the name of Jesus.

- I forgive my teacher who treated me badly in the name of Jesus Christ.

- I forgive the persons in my life who have hurt and rejected me in the name of Jesus Christ.

- I command the spirit of rejection to let me go and be loose from me. I bind you up in the name of Jesus and cast you out of my life to never return.

- I let go of the hurt I got from people in the name of Jesus Christ.

- I will not suffer any more from the past pain and hurt from family and people in the name of Jesus Christ.

- I command the spirit of hurt and pain to let me go, be loosed from me and I bind you up in the name of Jesus and cast you out of my life to never return.

  NOTE: It's a powerful and positive step to forgive those who have caused you pain. Your declaration of forgiveness is a personal and meaningful choice.

  Remember that forgiveness is a process, and it can contribute to your own healing and peace of mind.

  Find strength and solace in your faith and forgiving others, in the name of Jesus bring you comfort and grace.

Reflections

Dear Lord, I thank for Your guidance, strength, and healing. I trust in your love., mercy and wisdom to navigate relationships with forgiveness, understanding, and grace. Thank You for your unconditional love and for being my refuge in times of trouble. In Jesus' name, I pray. Amen.

Chapter Two

THE GENERATIONAL CURSE

"Christ redeemed us from the curse of the law by becoming a curse for us, for it is written: 'Cursed is everyone who is hung on a pole.' He redeemed us in order that the blessing given to Abraham might come to the Gentiles through Christ Jesus, so that by faith we might receive the promise of the Spirit." (Galatians 3:13-14 (NIV):

The adversary devised a wicked scheme for my life, and indeed, it was a dreadful one aimed at wreaking havoc from my early years. Little could anyone anticipate that an innocent girl like me would experience such trauma from such a tender age.

I had envisioned a future where I would joyfully walk down the aisle in a beautiful white dress, anticipating a life filled with happiness. I longed to experience the carefree joy of childhood, but unfortunately, that was stripped away from me.

I no longer take the blame.

My life changed the day that my Uncle Skinny started molesting me (see dictionary). Some of my family members never believed me. Some still will not believe or deny it even happened when they know the truth. Some never talk about it or even ask me about it.

Those who are not yet aware will now be informed about it. Growing up I felt guilty, but not anymore. I no longer blame myself for being molested.

I've never been alone.

Through everything I've endured, Jehovah, my God, has always been with me. Despite the challenges, I recognize that my Uncle Skinny or other male family members could have inflicted even greater harm. Gratitude fills my heart as I thank the Lord for His unwavering protection.

As a little girl, my love for dancing was undeniable, a passion that still resonates with me today. Whenever music played on the television, I couldn't resist the urge to get up and start dancing. Oddly, my Uncle Skinny would express disapproval, shouting at me to sit down. However, my grandmother, understanding my joy, would defend me, insisting that I be left alone.

In a household dominated by two uncles, a grandfather, and my grandmother, I was the sole little girl. During the day, my little cousins and a helper would join our household. Despite the familial setting, my love for music and dancing brought me immense happiness.

Strangely, it seemed as if my uncle couldn't bear to see me enjoying myself through dance. Simple clapping and jumping around would elicit a disapproving look, as if I were somehow a terrible person for finding joy in the rhythm of life.

My life was miserable, and I took it out on others.

We had an indoor bathroom and an outdoor pit toilet, so during the day, I used the outside facility.

One particular day, as I entered the toilet, my Uncle Skinny came

34

inside, and fear gripped me. I questioned his actions, and he forcefully pushed me against the side of the toilet shred.

The sensation of the spikes in the board piercing my skin was unimaginable. I pleaded with him to stop, threatening to tell Mama (grandmother).

In response, he callously asserted that she would never believe me. It struck me as ironic since he had witnessed Mama doubting and chastising me numerous times before, reinforcing the idea that she wouldn't believe my account.

Despite my tears, he finished the ordeal, enduring further indignity as he left a repugnant substance on my leg— resembling nose mucus. I cleaned myself up in silence, choosing not to confide in anyone about this painful incident.

I was afraid every time I wanted to use the toilet and I would look around to make sure he wasn't there, but he would for some reason come in after like he was hiding behind something watching.

My life was miserable, and I took it out on kids in school that wanted to be rude to me or hit me or hurt my family.

No one was protecting me at home so at school I protected others and myself. Whenever we would have sports event at my middle school and as I walked around campus in the night.

I would smell the nasty thing my Uncle Skinny left on me. I thought someone was doing that same thing to a girl.

I never forgot that smell.

I was confused and angry. I couldn't concentrate on my school, and I kept remembering what my Uncle Skinny did to me. Sad to say, I felt that I had been molested by other family members too, but in a different way.

Molestation is a Generational Curse

I found out years after that this time of Molestation was Incest a Generational Curse.

According to the Urban Dictionary *Incest means To engage in sexual activities with one who is of blood relations.*

> *"None of you shall approach any one of his close relatives to uncover nakedness. I am the Lord."* (Leviticus 18:6, ESV).

> *The Lord is against such an act. Even when King David's son raped his daughter and her other brother was full of wrath, but David did nothing. because it was wrong and against the law of God. (Read 2 Samuel 13).*

Navigating a situation were speaking out leads to repercussions and rights are lacking creates a difficult dilemma. During a visit from my male cousin named Whitey, who came from another city bearing gifts, I interpreted the gestures as genuine affection.

The joy of experiencing love, receiving hugs, and even a kiss on the cheek overwhelmed me. At that moment, I failed to recognize the wrongness of the situation, as I perceived it as an expression of care rather than mistreatment.

I knew something was wrong when he started touching my

genital area and my breasts. He asked if I was growing hair. He would take his private out of his pants, and grab my hand, make me touch it.

One time he had me go in the chicken pen with him and he touched my private. I went to use the toilet and saw something crawling on me. I was so frightened. Other times other male family members would touch my genital too. I never told anyone; I kept my mouth shut.

It's perplexing to me why, when I attempted to express my feelings in a letter, I ended up being physically harmed by three family members.

One Sunday my other molester, Whitey came with his half-brother, and I got a kiss from the half-brother. I started feeling something, but I couldn't quite comprehend it, so I decided to write it down. The half-brother seemed charming.

I expressed in the letter that I hoped the kind cousin wasn't upset about his half-brother kissing me. I struggled with these emotions, unsure of how to articulate them. After writing the letter, I crumpled the paper, as if releasing the emotions bottled up inside me.

The beatings and molestations appeared to be endless.

My, my, my! One of my uncles, Uncle Gray, who lived nearby, came to the house and saw me cleaning out my school bag.

I had some old crush papers in there, and he took them from me, reading the papers. Discovering the letter, he promptly informed my grandmother and my visiting aunt, Aunt Flowers.

In a distressing turn of events, Uncle Gray, a stern figure, along with my grandmother and Aunt Flowers, took turns beating me. It was a bewildering experience, being subjected to consecutive beatings without a clear explanation of my wrongdoing. They simply pointed to the letter and commenced the punishment.

Uncle Gray, who had discovered my letter, had never been fond of me, always exhibiting a mean demeanor and subjecting me to frequent beatings. It got to a point where my mother had to intervene, urging my grandmother to instruct Uncle Gray to cease beating her child.

The Molestation continues from my Uncle Skinny. A female cousin Sarah came to visit, and we would play hide and seek in the night. One of the rooms we would run into was the one my Uncle Skinny the molester sleeps in and another good uncle.

He arrived home while we were playing, and with the lights off in the room that had only a curtain instead of a door, I was unaware of his presence.

As I rushed into the dark room, I felt someone grab me.

Reacting instantly, I shouted, and he released his grip. Rushing outside, I warned my cousin Sarah not to enter the room because he was inside.

Sarah asked me why I told her to not go back inside and I told her how he was rubbing his sex organ on me. I confided in Sarah because I wanted to prevent what happened to me from

38

happening to her.

I had recently disclosed the same to my mother, who was exploring ways to have me live with her. Even though I was just a child and unaware at the time, God was helping me navigate through these challenging experiences.

One day, while I was at home, my Aunt Flowers visited us again. Sarah, who was residing with her at the time, confided in her about everything I told her. Upon receiving this information, Aunt Flowers called me, and when I joined her, both she and my grandmother were present.

Aunty Flowers said Sarah told her that my uncle was touching my genital area and doing things to me. In response, I affirmed what my cousin Sarah told our Aunty Flowers by saying, "Yes."

They contacted Uncle Skinny and inquired about the situation, to which he denied the allegations, claiming that I was lying. Despite my insistence on the truth, it seemed they were reluctant to believe me, echoing his previous statements from the times he had molested me.

I affirmed that my mother was aware of the truth since I had already informed her. They then instructed me to fetch my mother. Walking approximately a mile to her house, and back I shared the details with her.

My mother returned with me, confirming that I was telling the truth. Unfortunately, she couldn't take me in as she had no place for me to stay but said she would try to find a way for me to live with her.

I had to take matters into my own hands.

You would have thought that he would stop molesting me and my grandmother would protect me now that she knew.

Ohhhhh, no!

One evening, my grandmother left me alone in the house as she attended church service to oversee the barrels that had arrived from America.

She instructed me that whatever my two uncles took from the barrels and gave to me, I should report to her upon her return from church.

Even though my grandmother is no longer alive to speak for herself, I am confident that I am speaking the truth.

Uncle Skinny came and took things out of the barrel and then gave me something to not say anything then molested me in his room. I felt like the food barrels was better than me for I was left alone to be molested.

It was at that point that I began devising a plan to run away.

I was growing up. Eventually, he is going to realize that he is not inserting his male sex organ inside of me and when he does, he will get me pregnant. I prayed to God, asking for His help to prevent me from getting pregnant by my uncle. I devised a plan to run away to my mother's house, where I hoped to find refuge.

Recognizing that my grandmother's bed had storage at the foot, I packed my clothes in plastic bags. When the time came to run away, I would simply grab the bags and go.

I frequently sat and talked to God, and one Saturday, I made up my mind to run away.

In the middle of the day, I collected my bags filled with clothes and headed to the back of the yard, traversing my neighbor's backyard. Upon arriving in the backyard of a cousin.

I engaged in conversation with them just as I heard my grandmother calling my name. Swiftly, my cousin directed me to hide in their house.

When my grandmother arrived and questioned if they had seen me, they all replied in the negative. I felt a surge of happiness that they had provided a hiding place for me, fully cognizant of the mistreatment I experienced from my grandmother.

Several months before this incident, I had a friend who lived in this house. One day, on our way home, we were playing, and she accidentally pushed me. I fell and ended up with scratches on my body.

When I got home, my grandmother noticed the injuries and asked me what had happened. I explained the situation, and my grandmother became so upset that she took me to the same house where my friend was staying. She called my friend, along with her stepmother and other relatives who were present.

Once again, I narrated what had happened, and my grandmother threatened to beat me herself if anyone else dared to discipline me, and true to her word, she publicly administered a beating right in front of everyone. I cried and felt ashamed.

From that moment on, I vowed never to let anyone beat me or harm me again, and I refrained from retaliating in kind. I made it a point that in any disagreement, no one could claim they had beaten me.

After my grandmother left their house, I walked through another yard and through some bushes. Emerging on the street, I checked if I could walk, and as I strolled, I saw my grandfather, my mother's father, leaving his home. Curious, I asked him where he was going, and he informed me he was heading to my mother's house.

I hopped into the van with him, and he drove me to my mother's house where my grandmother was waiting for me. My grandmother had a conversation with my mother, and I ended up back at my grandmother's house.

Upon returning to my grandmother's house, she informed me that I would never see my mother again unless she accompanied me. Devastated by this, I made up my mind to run away once more. I couldn't bear the thought of enduring further molestation by men in her family, and, most importantly,

Will I ever see my mother again?

I refused to accept the reality of never being able to see my mother again.

I prayed to God for help because I wanted to see my mother. I prayed and asked Him to stop the molestation being done to me by my male family members. I cried and cried, seeking help, and formulated plans in my head. I was determined not to give up.

I packed my clothes in bags again, making sure to keep my church clothes in one place. I decided that one Saturday evening, when my grandmother decided to go to the area where my mother lived, I would run away again.

I couldn't wait for Saturday to come. We went to church to clean, and she mentioned that we would go to Soho (the district where my mother lived).

I was thrilled, thinking, "Now I can run away again."

I began planning in my head that I would mention needing to use the restroom, then run back through the shortcut to the house to gather my belongings.

The time came for us to go to Soho, and I asked if I could go to my mom's house to use the restroom. My grandmother sent one of my little boy cousins to follow me.

When we reached my mother's house and exchanged greetings with her and my sisters, I don't even recall if anyone else was there. I went to the outside toilet, and my cousin went inside the house.

I quietly passed by where my sisters were talking, sprinted to the road, ensuring no one spotted me. It was pitch dark, but I disregarded it. I was resolute on running away again.

You might wonder why I didn't just stay, considering I was at my mother's house. I needed my clothes for school, church, dresses, shoes, and other belongings. I wasn't running away with nothing, no way!

Though I couldn't retrieve my bank book, which was alright. Tired but on a mission, I observed my grandfather (who passed away years ago) watching television in the living room. Peeking at him, I took my things out of the room little by little.

The dogs were barking, and I attempted to quiet them. He heard sounds, checked through the window or opened the door, but he didn't see me.

I removed all my clothes from the closet, left the hangers on the bed, went to the back of the house, and the other dogs continued barking. These dogs were tied up because they were very aggressive.

I passed them and went to my neighbor's house, waiting there for a little while. My grandmother returned home with my little cousin.

I overheard her asking my grandfather about me, and he claimed not to know.

They checked the room and remarked that I left the hangers on the bed.

My neighbor, an older lady saw me standing in her yard with my things and heard what they were saying. She shook her head at me, and I continued to listen to grandmother talking about me.

My molester Uncle Skinny told my grandmother to kill me with a licking (beaten) when I come back.

Can you believe this man who wants to continue molesting me telling my grandmother to hurt me? He spoke angrily as he talked to my grandmother about me.

She mentioned that I was going to my mother's and her my grandmother intended to return to my mother's house. Unaware that I was still nearby, overhearing their plot against me. I firmly decided never to go back there, no matter what.

Once again, I saw my grandfather leaving his yard, and he asked if I was heading to my mother's. I confirmed, and he mentioned that he was going there to bring some bread to his mother. My mother, his daughter, served as the caretaker for his mother (her grandmother).

When I arrived at my mother's house, I found my grandmother sitting on the porch with my mother. Gathering my belongings, I approached them and informed my mother that I wouldn't be returning with my grandmother.

I recounted my grandmother's declaration that I would never see her again and Uncle Skinny's suggestion to 'kill me with beating.'

Despite my grandmother's objections, I asserted my decision, stating that I would rather sleep on the floor than return with her.

My mother, understanding the need to protect me from molestation and physical assault, agreed to let me stay. I remained firm in my resolve, indifferent to my grandmother's protests. We discussed sleeping arrangements.

I removed the board that was used to block the dogs from entering the porch and coming inside the house. I gave it to my mother, and she placed old clothes on it for me to have a comfortable sleep. Each morning, I would put it away.

I continued sleeping on this makeshift bed until my stepfather decided to bring his full-size bed, which he had before marrying my mom, and gave it to me. I was elated.

God touched his heart, and he showed kindness. He didn't have to, but he did. It's a testament that God will protect you and grant you favor with man.

"For thou, Lord, wilt bless the righteous; with favor wilt thou compass him as with a shield. (Psalms 5:12)

GOD NEVER LEFT ME ALONE.

He told me to runway to live with my mother to be safe. God had people help me both times I ran away. God guided me through the night going through the dark bushes.

I wasn't afraid because I didn't feel alone. God gave me a wisdom on how to pack my things and prepare to run away and what time to do it.

It's God and not me an 11-year-old little girl being sexually, mentally, and physically abused. God protects his children. I know I got molested but God prevented my uncle from getting me pregnant and doing worse things to me and even my other cousins. God had his hands on me and I'm blessed.

The spirit of incest followed me, and other male family members later were looking at me and I could feel their emotions towards me, and I had protected myself. I came to America to live with my dad who filed for me, and a male cousin started looking at me sexually.

I felt that feeling again. I knew something was wrong but who could I tell.

That incest curse was following me around. Every time I see him, I felt that weird feeling and one day he approached me, and I told him I will not have sex with him.

I was determined that no family member would have sex with me. It was like the incest spirit was drawing him towards me and he was curse too because his uncle and cousins molested me in

Jamaica.

I had to get away.

I was attending a business academy, and a military recruiter came by, and I did the pretest. I told my dad, and he said not join, but when I see what was going on and my cousin wanted to have sex with me, I said I have to run away again and this time I will learn to kill men and defend myself from abusers.

My parents weren't happy I wanted to join the US Army Reserve, but they had no idea why a smart 19-year-old wanted to be a soldier.

I just migrant to America in January 2003 and joined the block out day in New York August 2003. I was going to be free and learn to be a warrior and no man will ever sexually abuse me again.

Chapter Two

Child Safety Lessons

<u>PARENTS</u>

- Parents or guardians, refrain from engaging in physical or emotional abuse towards your children.

- Parents or guardians should exercise caution when dealing with individuals who habitually find fault with everything your child or children do.

- Parents or guardians should exercise caution when individuals give excessive attention to their child or children.

- Parents or guardians should exercise caution when individuals persistently give gifts to their child or children.

- Parents or guardians should exercise caution regarding how someone touches their child or children.

- Parents or guardians should take immediate action if your child reports inappropriate touching by someone. Investigate the matter and consider consulting a doctor for further guidance and support.

- Parents or guardians do not molest your own child or someone else's child.

- Parents or guardians, when administering discipline such as a spanking, communicate clearly with the child about the reason for the consequence and explain why the behavior should not be repeated.

- Seek prayer for your child to be delivered from the spirits of sexual, physical, and mental abuse. Invite the healing power of prayer to bring comfort, strength, and restoration to your child's mind, body, and spirit.

CHILDREN

- Children, it is important to be honest with your parents, even if you fear potential consequences. Open communication fosters trust and understanding in your relationship.

- Children do not be afraid of your abuser. It's crucial to speak up and confide in your parents, guardians, or someone you trust about any inappropriate actions or harm you may be experiencing. Your safety and well- being are of utmost importance.

- Children if your parents are molesting you tell someone that you trust.

Chapter Two

GENERATIONAL CURSE

"For He will command His angels concerning you, to guard you in all your ways." (Psalm 91:11)

❖ Lord, thank you for forgiving me as I took part in physical and sexual abuse.

❖ I renounce the spirit of physical, emotional, mental and sexual abuse from my life in the name of Jesus Christ.

❖ I forgive my abuser in the name of Jesus Christ.

❖ I renounce the spirit of abuse, molestation, incest and generation curse in the name of Jesus Christ.

❖ I command the spirit of (say the name of the abuse you had experience with) …. abuse, molestation, incest and generation curse to let me go and get out my body and life in the name of Jesus Christ.

❖ I bind up the spirit of incest, abuse, molestation and generational curse in the name of Jesus Christ.

❖ I send the spirit of incest, abuse, molestation and generational curse back to the pit of hell and never return to my body and life in the name of Jesus Christ.

❖ Thank you Lord I am free in the name of the Jesus Christ for your word said "John 8:36(KJV) "If the Son therefore shall make you free, ye shall be free indeed".

Lord, in your infinite wisdom and boundless love, we humbly ask for Your protection over our children. Surround them with Your angels and create a hedge of safety around them wherever they go.

Shield them from harm and danger, both seen and unseen.

Grant them the strength to resist negative influences and the courage to make wise choices. May Your light guide their path, illuminating the way in times of darkness. Keep them safe from accidents, illness, and all forms of harm.

We pray for the parents, caregivers, and all those who play a role in their lives. May they be filled with compassion, wisdom, and patience as they nurture and guide our children.

Lord, we also lift up all the children around the world who are facing difficult circumstances.

Whether it be due to poverty, violence, or any form of injustice, we pray for Your intervention and protection. Bring comfort to those who are hurting and hope to those who are in despair.

Most importantly, help us, as parents, guardians, and caregivers, to be vigilant and responsible stewards of the precious lives You've entrusted to us.

Grant us the wisdom to lead by example, teaching them Your ways and instilling in them a deep sense of love and faith. We place our children into Your loving hands, trusting that Your watchful care will always be with them. In Jesus' name, we pray. Amen.

Reflections

Dear Heavenly Father, we come before You with hearts full of gratitude for the precious gift of children that You have entrusted to our care. We recognize that they are truly a blessing from You, and we thank You for the joy and love they bring into our lives.

Chapter Three

RAPE, MY DEATH

Living with my mother and attending high school made me feel content, safe and happy. I was free from being molested and treated unfairly.

Attending high school parties, making new friends, and participating in sports events were enjoyable experiences. My mother permitted us to attend these events, but with the condition that we return home early; she was careful about us being out late at night.

Dancing, in particular, became a source of joy and liberation, providing a welcome escape from the pain and hurt I had experienced. It was a way to break free from the cycle of hurt that one negative experience could lead to another.

Being molested opened up my body for other spirits to possess, oppressed me and bring destruction to my life.

One day, I went shopping for clothing to wear to a dancing event at my high school. I wasn't familiar with the street vendors selling clothes, but I usually bought whatever caught my eye. Despite being old enough to shop on my own, this particular day proved different.

Unable to find what I was looking for, a male vendor suggested he had more items in a nearby building.

Suddenly, my usual sense of awareness seemed to slip away. I found myself following him, my mind momentarily not my own. He engaged in conversation with a lady and motioned for me to join. Although a strange feeling crept over me, I continued to follow him unquestioningly.

His instructions, like crossing the street, were obeyed without hesitation. He then suggested we walk by the beach, and I went along without resistance.

Deep down, I sensed that something was amiss, but I couldn't shake the strange trance-like state I was in. As we walked, it became apparent that there was no store where he was leading me.

Despite being fully aware of my surroundings, an inexplicable inability to say no to this man held me captive. He instructed me to return home and come back later for the clothing I desired.

Instead of asserting myself and choosing another vendor, I obediently went home. While there, I couldn't shake the feeling that the man was dishonest, yet an irresistible compulsion drew me back to him.

In the evening, as he had suggested, I returned to the city. Locating him, he insisted that I follow him to a building where he claimed to have the shorts I had been searching for.

The persistence of his request and the mysterious hold it had over me continued to bewilder and trouble my thoughts. Upon reaching the building, a persistent unease lingered in my thoughts, whispering that something was amiss. In the dimly lit surroundings, I inquired about the location of the clothes.

Suddenly, I felt a force pushing me down onto a bench. The man positioned himself on top of me, repeatedly muttering that someone was approaching.

Confused and frightened, I demanded him to release me, questioning why he was hiding if this was supposedly his storage space.

The weight of the man pressed down on me, and a sense of weakness overwhelmed me. Desperation took hold, and I screamed for help, my pleas echoing in the darkness. However, my cries seemed to fall on deaf ears, as no one came to my aid.

The isolation and vulnerability of that moment became hauntingly apparent.

He began lifting my skirt, and I relentlessly pushed him away, but he ended up raping me, anyway. His huge body was on top of me raping me. He insisted that I cease screaming and resisting, asserting that no one would hear or come to my rescue.

In tears, I wiped away the evidence of my distress, straightened my disheveled clothes after he eventually let go. I went to the taxi stand, got a taxi and went home.

The Ordeal Left Me Feeling Out of Touch with Reality

Once home, I sought solace in a shower before heading to the dance event. In search of my boyfriend, I queried his friends, but the details of that night remain blurred as shock gripped me.

I refrained from dancing, instead, watching others in a daze. The ordeal left me feeling detached and out of touch with reality.

Feeling unwell, I eventually visited the clinic where I often saw pregnant women. There, I confided in the nurse, expressing my desire to undergo a pregnancy test. The results came back positive.

I cried and told her I don't want the baby because a man had raped me. Overwhelmed and unsure of what to do, I took a seat.

After a period of uncertainty, the nurse summoned me and

suggested an IUD, explaining that it could prevent the development of the pregnancy. Relieved to have a solution, I agreed to proceed with the IUD.

Only God knew how much my vagina was hurting from the IUD. I was in so much pain and bleeding that I thought "Okay, the egg is broken down, just few more days and the pain will be over."

I was going through torture but, oh it was worth it. At least that was what I thought. It was a long weekend and on Monday at school I couldn't take it anymore.

It felt like something was ripping my vagina inside apart. Like literally it was a sharp pain and sticking me.

I asked for an excuse to go to the clinic near my school and I told the nurse my situation and that I wanted the IUD removed. The doctor told me that my uterus was too small and that is why the IUD was hurting me much.

My vagina felt so much better after the IUD was removed and the bleeding stopped.

Now I wasn't pregnant, and I can go on with my life and on one else will ever know that I had gotten raped. I started feeling weird. I hated how the flowers in my yard smelled and made me sick to the stomach... I found myself wanting to sleep a lot.

Something is Wrong

Something must be wrong with me, and I had to find a way to tell my boyfriend. One day, while visiting him at his house I told him that I was pregnant, and the baby was his.

He said, "No, it couldn't be because we always use a condom.

I reminded him of the night at the high school dance party. I told him that I had taken off walking looking for him. I began crying as I shared how a man grabbed me and forced himself on me.

Looking at him with tears running down my face; anticipating his reaction as I said, "I got raped earlier in the Morant Bay."
I told him the story of how it happened and the IUD procedure. He said he would go find the man and killed him for raping me.

I said, "No it's not worth you going to jail for what someone else did."

Shaking his head in anger; he said that his dad had a gun, and it was licensed. I could tell he was thinking about getting his father's gun and looking for the guy who had raped me.

Towards the end of our conversation, he reached over and rubbed my belly. He felt a bulge and said he could tell that I was pregnant.

Lifting up my blouse he said, "I don't know if you ever heard of this, but the black mark going down a lady's belly gets darker when she is pregnant."

Bending and looking even closer at my stomach, he said. "Yes, you are pregnant."

The Search

I feel like my life is about to end. I can't tell my parents what happened. On top of that, I will be disgraced by the people in my community. I didn't know what to do so I went searching for the man that raped me at the shopping center.

What I found out was devastating. A man told me that the person I am looking for has been working witchcraft on females and raping them, but he isn't getting caught.

I asked him did he knew where the man lived but he said, he didn't know. A thought came to mind, and he said, he knew someone who may know and he sent me to a shop where he felt someone could help me.

I was so desperate to find this man and I went alone after the person at the shop told me where the man that raped me lived.

I didn't stop to think. The thought never came to my mind that I could be in danger or that that he could kill, hurt or rape me again. My only thought was to find this guy and make him give me money to get an abortion.

One Sunday afternoon, while my mother was at church, I decided I would go look for him because I needed money to have the abortion. I asked one of my older sisters to tell my mother that she sent me to run an errand for her.

When I arrived at the place where the shopkeeper told me the man lived; I asked a few people in the neighborhood of his whereabouts. I was there for hours until it was getting dark. Finally, I saw him at the bus stop.

I walked up to him and before he could say anything; I said, "You raped me. I didn't go to the police and now I am pregnant. I need money to have an abortion."

Can you believe that this man said I had to have sex with him in order to get the money for an abortion?

I was angry and outraged. I yelled loudly; "I will not."
I kept asking and asking and it was getting late, and I knew my mother would be looking for me.

This time, I managed to break free from his mind-control powers, and he couldn't control me any longer.

It was late, and I felt lost and injured, uncertain about what to do since I hadn't obtained the money. Additionally, my father is in the process of filing for me to move to America, and facing the prospect of going there pregnant is causing me distress.

My mother doesn't have any room for me and a baby conceived from rape and I wasn't going to raise a rapist's baby. My child wasn't going to be called a rapist child his or her entire life and we both live in shame.

An Angel

I yearned for a good life without becoming the subject of gossip, but the question lingered: who would believe my story? Desperate and confused, I prayed for guidance, asking God for direction on what to do and how to face my parents, knowing I couldn't go home pregnant.

Standing at the bus stop, a sudden thought struck me as I gazed at a colossal bridge spanning over rushing waters. I walked to the middle, gripping the rails and peering down at the tumultuous stream below. The idea of jumping off crossed my mind – a desperate attempt to escape and disappear, my body forever lost in the relentless current.

Just as I was about to climb the rails and succumb to the darkness, a man's voice intervened with a stern 'Don't do it.' I released my grip on the rails, turning toward the direction of the voice. In the dim light, I could barely discern a man, his face obscured. Glancing back at the river, I reconsidered my actions.

As I retraced my steps to the bus stop, I scanned my surroundings for the mysterious voice, but he remained unseen.

Upon reaching the bus stop, I inquired with a lady if she had seen the man, but she claimed she hadn't. Puzzled, I wondered how the man had vanished so swiftly, considering he had been right beside me just a few minutes before at the bridge.

As I waited for a taxi to take me home, I kept contemplating my desperate situation. I never disclosed my thoughts of self-harm to anyone, grappling with the belief that no one could offer the help I needed.

Unbeknownst to me, God was looking out for me, a realization that came later. Despite feeling utterly alone, a verse from Hebrews 13:5 echoed in my mind, reassuring me that I was not abandoned:

"I will never leave you nor forsake you."

Reflecting on my contemplation of suicide, I acknowledge the difficulty I faced in reaching out to my parents or family for support. At that moment, ending my own life seemed like the only solution to avoid the challenges of an unwanted pregnancy. It's a dark place to be, and if you're still struggling, consider seeking assistance from a mental health professional or confiding in someone you trust. There are people and resources available to help you navigate through difficult times.

I found myself listening to the negative voice urging me to jump off the bridge. The persistent thoughts of suicide seemed to surface whenever something terrible occurred or when I felt overwhelmingly alone.

It seemed as though nobody truly knew or cared enough to reach out to me. From my childhood onward, I've been confronted with a series of unfortunate events, and as a teenager, it felt like nothing had changed. I questioned the purpose of continuing to live.

Reflecting on that dark time, I'm grateful for God's love, evident in what I believe was the intervention of His angel to prevent me from taking that drastic step.

If I had succumbed to those thoughts, I wouldn't be here speaking to you now or experiencing the achievements in my life, which I attribute to my faith in Christ Jesus.

Chapter Three

<u>Lessons on Rape</u>

God condemns acts of violence, including rape. For instance, the Bible strongly advocates for love, respect, and kindness towards others. It states in Ephesians 5:25 (NIV):

"Husbands, love your wives, just as Christ loved the church and gave himself up for her."

This passage emphasizes loving and respecting one another, which stands in stark contrast to the act of rape that involves harm, violation, and disrespect.

- There is a belief that individuals might employ witchcraft to manipulate and exert control over others, leading to abusive situations.

- Suicide is not the answer to difficult things.

- Always avoid going anywhere with someone unfamiliar to you.

- Stay vigilant, carefully assessing both your companions and your surroundings.

- Never let your guard down because you want to gain materials things.

- Pray and ask God to direct your daily steps and protect you from the traps of the devil.

- Seek help from others when you don't know how to handle a problem.

- Reject negative thoughts about yourself.

- Seek medical care after an unwanted sexual act to ensure you don't get pregnant.

- Report unwanted sex to the police and others you trust.

- Never blame yourself for an assault based on the clothes you wear or your feelings towards someone.

- Extend a helping hand to others you observe getting into precarious situations that may lead to harm or rape.

- God will send His angels to protect you from danger or death.

Chapter Three

Rape & Suicide

❖ I forgive myself for getting rape.

❖ I forgive my rapist in the name of Jesus Christ.

❖ I renounce the spirit of mind control, rape and suicide in the name of Jesus Christ.

❖ I lose myself from the spirit of mind control, rape and suicide in the name of Jesus Christ.

❖ I bind the spirit of mind control, rape and suicide in the name of Jesus Christ.

❖ I cast out the spirit of mind control, rape and suicide out of my body and life in the name of Jesus Christ.

❖ The spirit of mind control, rape and suicide will not return to my life nor follow me around in the name of Jesus Christ.

❖ I reject negative thoughts about myself in the name of Jesus.

❖ My Heavenly Father Jehovah loves me and I will survive the hurt in the name of Jesus Christ.

❖ Jesus Christ has set me free, and I am free indeed from the spirt of mind control, rape and suicide.

❖ I will no longer live in fear of being rape again in the name of Jesus Christ.

❖ I will longer live in fear of wanting to kill myself after any bad situation in my life in the name of Jesus Christ of Nazareth.

❖ My Lord and Savior Jesus Christ has made me whole.

Reflections

Dear Heavenly Father, I come before You in humility and thanking you for Your divine intervention and protection. I acknowledge Your sovereignty and power over all things.

Lord, I thank you for my deliverance from these dark forces that seek to harm and destroy. Thank you for covering me with Your protective grace and surround me with Your heavenly angels to guard against the schemes of darkness.

Thank you for letting me see the value of my life and the purpose You have for me. For healing the wounds inflicted by thoughts of assault and suicide, and restoring my mental and emotional well-being

I declare Your promises from Psalm 34:17-18:

"The righteous cry out, and the Lord hears them; he delivers them from all their troubles. The Lord is close to the brokenhearted and saves those who are crushed in spirit." Thank you, Heavenly Father, for Your unfailing love and mercy. In Jesus' name, I pray. Amen.

Chapter Four

MY PAIN

"The Lord is close to the brokenhearted and saves those who are crushed in spirit." Psalm 34:18 (NIV*):*

Facing an unexpected pregnancy, I felt overwhelmed and uncertain about what to do. Desperate for assistance, my only confidant was my boyfriend.

He took it upon himself to search for an abortion doctor in our city, revealing a daunting cost of $4,000 – a sum neither of us could afford, especially since he was unemployed, and I was still in high school.

In an attempt to help, my boyfriend pledged to contribute. $2,000, leaving me responsible for the remaining $2,000. Faced with this financial burden, I grappled with the challenge of obtaining the money.

Reluctant to seek assistance from my family or anyone else, I found myself in a difficult position, compelled to navigate the complexities of securing funds for the abortion.

In the midst of this crisis, I questioned how I would gather the necessary funds, feeling isolated and without a support network.

The prospect of asking for financial help weighed heavily on me, and I was left with the distressing task of figuring out a solution, driven by the urgent need for the funds required.

In this tumultuous time, I can't recall if I turned to prayer, but my primary focus was on obtaining the necessary funds for the abortion procedure.

I found myself in a state of depression, anxiety, and confusion. The weight of my situation became a heavy burden that I couldn't share with my family or classmates.

As the days passed, I struggled to concentrate in class and prepare for final exams. The exhaustion was overwhelming, to the point where, on days with afternoon classes, I would get dressed for school only to take a nap due to overwhelming sleepiness.

Certain foods, particularly a tin of meat called Mackerel, became intolerable, evoking nausea with its smell and taste. Even a flower in my yard triggered a physical reaction, making me feel sick.

One day at school, I discovered my blouse was wet, realizing that my breasts were leaking milk. To manage this, I resorted to putting tissues in my blouse to absorb any leakage.

My cravings intensified, leading me to indulge in specific food combinations, such as ice cream and putting banana chips in a beef patty.

The cravings even extended to a desire for ice, to the point where my boyfriend cautioned me about being discreet to avoid unwanted attention.

I faced challenges in staying awake during classes, often

succumbing to drowsiness and sleep. The constant need to spit became a source of frustration, adding to the difficulties I was experiencing during this trying period.

I didn't like the life I was living because I got raped. I started praying more to God for help.

While at school, there was a mathematics teacher named Mr. Black who resided on campus and was popular among the girls. I thought he was sleeping with them for they were by his house a lot.

One day, he approached me and inquired about how I was doing, noticing the change in my attitude. I opened up to him, sharing my sorrowful story, and he expressed a genuine willingness to help.

When it was time for me to go to the clinic for checkups, he ensured I had the necessary passes to leave and return. I attributed his assistance to a higher power, acknowledging that, without God, he wouldn't have extended his help.

Even though I knew I was going to have the abortion I made sure that I was still healthy. During that challenging time, I clung to a glimmer of hope, believing that God was on my side, and it prevented me from sinking into complete despair.

Conversations with my compassionate teacher provided a sense of relief during my desperate state.

As my pregnancy progressed, I still lacked the $2,000 needed for the abortion.

Faced with financial difficulties, I found myself resorting to a regrettable coping mechanism. Men expressed interest and asked me out, and in an effort to obtain the money I needed, I engaged in sweet talk, prompting them to offer to buy me lunch, clothes, or other items.

Although I took the money with the intention of going out with them, deep down, I knew I had no intention of following through. Unfortunately, I became entangled in a deceitful pattern, essentially acting as a con artist to secure the funds necessary for my abortion.

It's important to note that I never engaged in any intimate relationships for money; rather, I took a risk by accepting financial assistance from these men.

During this challenging period, I felt a conflict between my desperation for financial relief and the moral implications of my actions.

Despite my choices, I believed that God was protecting me, allowing me to navigate these difficult circumstances.

However, I couldn't shake the profound question of why I had to endure such suffering and what I might have done to deserve this challenging situation.

What Will Become of my Life?

I was molested then rape and now going to have an abortion. What will my life become? As I gently caressed my belly, I engaged in conversations with my unborn child, expressing love and kindness.

The prospect of a baby growing inside me prompted deep contemplation about the future and what my life might evolve into.

I grappled with questions about the path ahead and the responsibilities that come with nurturing a life within. The uncertainty of this journey led me to reflect on the choices and decisions that lay before me as I navigated the complexities of motherhood.

As one month turned into two, the duration of my pregnancy weighed heavily on my mind. In moments of desperation, I found solace in tears and prayers to God, my only confidant who truly understood the turmoil within.

The urgency to address my situation intensified as my father's plans for our migration to America approached. Revealing my pregnancy would jeopardize this opportunity for a better life.

Faced with the challenge of not having financial support, I resolved to accumulate enough funds to spare myself from interactions with men I neither liked nor wanted to be with. The prospect of securing a better future and avoiding potential dangers was my driving force.

Despite the difficulties, I recognized the grace of God in protecting me from adverse outcomes. It was a relief that I did not have to resort to selling my body for financial support, sparing me from feelings of discomfort and disgust associated with such actions.

Now in January, I finally had the money. Gratefully, I thought to myself, thanking God for this provision. I informed my boyfriend that I had the necessary funds, and he contributed his share to support me through this difficult time. I felt a profound sense of gratitude for his assistance during this challenging period.

Contemplating his help, I wondered if he did so to avoid any association with the child if I decided to carry it. Regardless, I appreciated his support.

He provided me with the location of the doctor, and after careful consideration, I chose to schedule the procedure for a Thursday.

Nervous and uncertain about what would transpire, I couldn't shake the thought that the doctor would remove the baby, and I would go back to school the next day, bleeding and changed.

The weight of my decision weighed heavily on me, and I found myself praying for guidance, knowing that I was on the brink of making a significant and irreversible choice.

The words from Exodus 20:13(KJV),

"Thou shalt not kill,"

echoed in my mind.

Entering the doctor's office, I was met with kindness and friendliness. When he inquired about the reason for my visit, I explained that I had been a victim of rape. The doctor asked if I had reported it to the police, and I replied in the negative.

He diligently noted down the details of my experience.

Following our conversation, he explained that he would administer an injection in my buttock, a process that would take some hours to work and break down the fetus.

I Feel Horrible Inside

By the calculation of when I got rape, he said I'm two and half months. I felt horrible inside about being there, but I had no choice.

After the procedure, feeling hungry, I bought a variety of snacks and juice. Upon returning to my neighborhood, I found my boyfriend at his store. I shared the details of what had happened, and he warned me that the pain might manifest later.

Despite his prediction, I spent several hours with him, consuming the snacks and juices without feeling any immediate discomfort. Eventually, I went home in the night, having not informed my mother about my whereabouts that morning.

Upon arriving home, I found my mother and older sister engaged in conversation with a cousin. I greeted them, and my mother mentioned that food was left for me. Feeling the need to use the outdoor toilet due to its being late and dark, I grabbed a portable chimney.

While passing feces, I unexpectedly started vomiting through my nose, a shocking and alarming experience. All the snacks and juices seemed to be exiting my body simultaneously, and I silently prayed for help, feeling a sense of distress. After cleaning up, I went to bed.

The next morning, my mother informed me that she had heard me moaning in my sleep as if in pain. Although I wasn't experiencing pain, I decided not to go to school after hearing an inner voice suggesting otherwise.

As I prepared to lie down, the same voice instructed me to "put a towel on the bed," which I promptly did.

 Moments later, as I sat on the bed, I felt a sudden burst, and water soaked my shorts and the towel. I thought to myself, 'my water broke.' Reacting swiftly, I rushed outside to the pit toilet.

I found myself thinking, "Oh my, the baby is going to come out now." Squatting on the toilet, I pushed, and to my shock, a little fetus emerged. Witnessing its tiny hands, feet, and forming face left me in disbelief.

As I touched it, it slipped into the toilet. Alongside, large blood clots were expelled. In the dimly lit toilet, I strained to see the fetus, but it was too dark. I remained in that position until the flow of blood subsided.

The weight of what I had done hit me, and I cried for days.
Each year, during the month when I had the abortion, Mother's Day, or the anticipated birth date, I spiraled into deep depression. These occasions made me withdraw, avoiding conversation and any activities.

Witnessing pregnant women or newborns became a source of trauma, intensifying my self-loathing. I questioned whether I could ever bear a child. Then, a man of God prophesied that I would have a son in the future.

While this brought hope, the depression lingered, and I wondered if remnants of the abortion marked me.

Were there scars or tears in my organs, impacting my ability to have a child without complications? These questions haunted me until the man of God's prophecy offered a glimmer of reassurance.

I Have to Forgive Myself

It took me years to forgive myself for the abortion, a journey marked by healing and self-acceptance. The fear of experiencing a similar situation haunted me, leading me to take precautions after every sexual encounter.

I regularly took pregnancy tests to confirm that I wasn't pregnant, and at times, resorted to using the morning-after pill for added reassurance.

This fear became all-encompassing, making me paranoid about the possibility of another unwanted pregnancy.

Even when I was on birth control pills, I struggled to trust their effectiveness and doubted their ability to prevent pregnancy.

I was raped and I made a choice. I committed murder and now, I must carry the weight of knowing that my child is gone because of my actions. The absence of a proper burial for my child adds to the burden. Every year, I find myself calculating how old my child would be, haunted by the void left behind.

In the past, I used to dream of a little boy, playing and interacting with him in my dreams, bringing me joy.

He would call me mommy. However, with newfound understanding and spiritual growth, I realized the significance of such dreams, especially when they involved deceased children. Through prayer and seeking spiritual guidance, I managed to release myself from the grip of my dead son.

The Spirit of Death Walked with Me

The impact of the spirit of abortion extended beyond sorrow, depression, and pain. It manifested in various areas of my life, leading to the continual abandonment of projects and courses, as if things were being aborted before completion.

The spirit of death seemed to walk with me, causing miscarriages when I got married.

Other spiritual battles surrounded my pregnancies, and the spirit of abortion played a significant role. It became evident that the repercussions of abortion weren't limited to the physical act; they extended to my spiritual well-being.

By engaging in abortion, I unknowingly allowed other aspects of my life to be aborted, giving the spirit of death access to my existence. It felt like I had sacrificed my first child to the devil, opening demonic realms that affected not only my present but also the potential future of my unborn children.

I had unintentionally granted the devil the authority to snatch away my fetuses before they could fully develop.

I also found myself spiritually connected to a familiar child from the devil.

While my child's spirit was with the Lord, the devil played tricks on my mind. I fervently prayed against the influence of both the deceased child and the spiritual child. Seeking deliverance, I reached out to the Lord's servant, who prayed for me to break the strongholds in my life.

As a result, I no longer engage in visions of playing or conversing with a little boy or other spiritual children. The depression triggered by the sight of babies, my son's birthday month, or the anniversary of the abortion has lifted.

Through prayer and the acceptance of God's forgiveness, I have forgiven myself, aligning with the wisdom of Luke 6:37, "...forgive, and ye shall be forgiven." Understanding that forgiveness is not only for others but also for ourselves is a crucial step.

Without Self-Forgiveness, Expecting God's

Forgiveness Becomes A Challenging Task.

Chapter Four

"My Pain"

<u>Lessons</u>

- Abortion is murder because you are taking a life.

- Abortion can lead to mental illness, PTSD, depression, anxiety and cause sleepless nights.

- Abortion can cause you to live in fear of never getting pregnant again.

- Abortion takes away your joy and peace of mind.

- Abortion can damage your womb and reproductive organs leaves a physical, mental and spiritual scar.

- **Adoption** is another option for **Abortion.**

- Consider your decision carefully before proceeding with an abortion, and it's advisable to consult with medical professionals for guidance.

- If you are raped or molested, seek a doctor and to wash out the sperm from your womb to prevent the egg from becoming fertilized.

- Seek therapy after an abortion.

- If you have had an abortion please pray against the spirit of abortion, murder, mental illness, hurt, suicide, rejection, and pain.

- Avoid harboring self-hatred; instead, practice self-forgiveness and extend forgiveness to the person who got you pregnant.

- Rebuke every child you see in your dream calling you mother or you dream that you are breast feeding once you confirm with God that this wasn't the future, He was showing you.

Chapter Four

PAIN

❖ My Lord Jehovah I received your forgiveness me for having an abortion and killing my baby.

❖ Lord I'm sorry for not trusting in you to take care of me when I unexpectedly got pregnant.

❖ I renounce my relationship with the spirit of abortion and murder in the name of Jesus Christ.

❖ I terminate the contract I have with the spirit of abortion and murder in the name of Jesus Christ.

❖ I bind up the spirit of abortion and murder operating in my body and life in the name of Jesus Christ.

❖ I lose myself from the spirit of abortion and murder operating in my body and life in the name of Jesus Christ.

❖ I cast out the spirit of abortion and murder out of my body and life in the name of Jesus Christ.

- ❖ You spirit of abortion and murder will not return to my body and life in the name of Jesus Christ.

- ❖ Thank you, Jesus Christ, I am free from the spirit of abortion and murder.

- ❖ I place my body and life in the hands of my Heavenly Father in the name of Jesus Christ.

- ❖ **Repeat the same prayer for mental illness, PTSD from abortion, hurt, suicide, rejection, pain, and spiritual children.**

- ❖ I pray that nothing else will be aborted in my life in the name of Jesus Christ.

Reflections

Dear Lord Jehovah, I come before you with a heavy heart, thanking you for your forgiveness for the choice I made to have an abortion and end the life of my baby. I acknowledge the weight of this decision and the pain it has caused.

Please, Lord, I'm sorry for my actions, and grant me the strength to forgive myself. I seek your mercy and healing as I navigate through the consequences of my choices.

In your infinite compassion, guide me on a path of healing and restoration. Help me find peace in your forgiveness and grace. May your love surround me, providing comfort and assurance that I am forgiven.

I surrender my burdens to you, trusting in your mercy and knowing that your love surpasses all understanding. In Jesus' name, I pray. Amen.

THE POISON

I used to enjoy consuming alcoholic beverages, particularly the fruity ones. Whenever I attended events, I found comfort in drinking alcohol, as it provided a sense of relaxation and calmness.

Despite being aware of the negative after-effects, such as feeling tipsy, drowsy, or talkative, I would indulge in these drinks. There were occasions when I would discreetly let the effects wear off without letting others know.

One notable incident occurred during a Christmas Eve Grand Market dance, where I consumed an excessive amount of Jamaican Red Label Wine.

To my dismay, I became so intoxicated that I had to ask an unfamiliar man to accompany me to the bus stop. This serves as a reminder of how alcohol can lead to recklessness and trouble for some individuals.

I vividly recall boarding the bus, only to pass my house, and my ex-boyfriend, who happened to be driving and noticed my continued presence on the bus.

Concerned for my well-being, he stopped the vehicle and requested another friend, who was the conductor and known to me, to ensure my safe journey home.

In a haze, I found myself sitting in the middle of the street, and my friend, the conductor, kindly walked me home.

The next morning, I woke up in bed, still wearing the same clothes. Reflecting on that night, I realized it was unwise to consume alcohol, especially as I was upset about my boyfriend not attending the dance.

A few years after the incident, during the summer, I had arranged to spend the weekend at a Christian friend's house. However, upon arrival, she was absent, and when we reached out to her, she confessed to forgetting about my visit and that of my stepsister.

In reaction, I reached out to my male friend, Indian, who came to pick me up, and together we decided to go out. Eventually, I returned home for the remainder of the summer.

While at home during a holiday, I found myself seated when the house phone suddenly rang, prompting me to answer it. A man on the other end expressed his desire to make love to me. Irritated and not recognizing the voice, I responded curtly.

After hanging up, I realized it was my boyfriend, Captain. I called him back to confirm, and he admitted it was him.

He had planned to request time off to visit me, but my initial response deterred him, and he decided against it. Despite my explanation and apology, he remained firm, and I felt a surge of anger.

Pondering what to do, I heard a voice telling me, "Indian is going to call you and say that when you all go out, my sister and her boyfriend will go somewhere, leaving me at his house for a while until they come back. But I must say no, I won't stay at his house; I will go with my sister."

Agreeing to the voice, I waited, and sure enough, Indian called, conveying the exact words the voice had foretold. I stood my ground, saying no, and Indian accepted my decision without argument.

I Began Trusting Men Again

Occasionally, on weekends, I would go out with my sister, Curly, her boyfriend, Shortie, and their male friend, Indian, who eventually became my friend as well.

Indian later expressed his feelings for me, and unfortunately, I made the mistake of revealing that I was dating a married man serving in the Jamaican Defense Force.

Unbeknownst to me, Indian became jealous, and our interactions, which included phone conversations and visits to his house, took a dark turn.

Indian harbored malicious intentions towards me during the times we partied and danced together, all while I found comfort in his seemingly good nature. Having experienced rape a few years prior, I had just started trusting men again.

Returning to that holiday night, despite my lingering anger towards my boyfriend, I decided to go out. Curly mentioned we were heading to a club in Portland, and I eagerly anticipated a night out, remembering the fun we had had on previous occasions.

In the club, I danced with Indian and enjoyed some red label wine. The alcohol's effects only became apparent when I stopped dancing and began the journey home. I fell asleep in the car and woke up at Indian's house.

With a strong urge to urinate, I asked if I could use his bathroom, forgetting the warning the Lord had given me about this man. The influence of alcohol clouded my memory, leading to potential trouble, all while I only sought a restroom.

Indian allowed me into his house, and I headed to the bathroom. While using the toilet, I heard loud music playing, and I began to feel incredibly weak, struggling to stand.

Curious about the whereabouts of my sister and his friend, I asked Indian, and he informed me that they had left and gone elsewhere.

Drunk and disoriented, I questioned why and staggered towards the door, where the music blared loudly.

Attempting to open the door, I found it unyielding. I pleaded for him to open it, but instead, he turned the music up even louder.

As I persisted in my efforts, he grabbed a knife and advanced toward me, instructing me to remove my clothes.

Firmly refusing, I shouted for help, but he pressed the knife against my throat, insisting that I comply.

I pleaded for him not to rape me. Before he started raping me, I said, "Please don't rape me. I will give you oral sex, please don't."

This man said, "Yeah you don't want me, it's a married man you want."

During him raping me I shouted for my mother and God to help me. I was so weak I couldn't fight. I just kept shouting for God and saying not again not again staring at the window to my right.

I don't remember how long he raped me or how I got my clothes back on. I only recall getting in the car when my sister returned. The details of the conversation between us and what was said remain hazy.

Shortie dropped me off at home, and I sat on the veranda until daylight.

Eventually, I mustered the courage to call my boyfriend and informed him that I had been assaulted once again. He inquired whether I had reported the incident to my mother, the police, or my sister, to which I replied in the negative.

In a daze, I walked to where my sister, Curly, was at her boyfriend's house and shared the traumatic experience with them.

They expressed shock, explaining that Indian had informed them that I wanted to stay with him for a while, so they left and returned later. Stunned by the revelation, I returned home, and my mother was already aware of the situation, as my boyfriend had informed her during the call.

I was so Ashamed.

I was advised to see a doctor, so I returned to the same doctor who had performed my previous abortion. When I explained that I had been raped again, his reaction was one of disbelief.

After a moment of silence, he took my statement and proceeded to examine me. During the examination, he discovered some of the perpetrator's sperm inside me and took steps to cleanse me.

Feeling a deep sense of shame, I returned home to find the police and my mother engaged in conversation in the yard. I shared the details of the incident with them, and they inquired about my preferred course of action.

While unsure of who had contacted the police, it's possible that my boyfriend had made the call.

We didn't want the community to know so we didn't press charges against my rapist. Indian; my rapist, was told to give me money for my torn clothes and stay away from me. I never got any money from him.

If I had taken him to court, he would have gone to jail for I had evidence of him raping me. He didn't deny it to the police, which proved that I wasn't lying about him planning to and raping me.

For a few weeks I kept seeing him passing by my home. Shortie, his friend had stopped speaking to him. It came to a point that no one saw Indian again or heard about him. He just vanished.

I used to wonder if someone killed him. I wished he would die too but had to ask God to forgive me because him God will take

95

vengeance for me.

God's word said:

"Dearly beloved, avenge not yourselves, but rather give place unto wrath: for it is written, Vengeance is mine; I will repay, saith the Lord".

I felt so stupid and wanted to die because I couldn't believe I had allowed myself to get raped again.

Even though my boyfriend and I had been dating for months, we hadn't engaged in sexual activity yet. I was waiting until I felt comfortable being intimate with him. Unfortunately, my trust in him led to a traumatic experience.

I questioned why these things happened to me, and I developed a strong aversion to anything related to sex. It became a struggle for me to cope with intimacy, and I found it difficult to let my boyfriend touch me.

He, however, was patient, understanding, and offered valuable advice. Despite his support, I harbored self-hatred and resentment towards men.

Depression set in, and I continually asked God why such misfortunes befell me. Feeling unloved by my family and facing a lack of job opportunities after graduating, I yearned for something positive in my life. Although I participated in enjoyable activities, inwardly, I was deteriorating.

I kept my feelings hidden, fearing judgment if I were to share them. It seemed challenging to discuss, and I felt foolish.

Negative thoughts about myself, men, and life plagued my mind.

Who would care about what happened to me and truly understand my experience? I was the one who was raped, not them.

How can I be certain that I won't face rape again? Was I being punished for something I did? I felt scared and decided to take matters into my own hands to protect myself.

It is Time to Make a Move

Although moving to America was a positive change, I found myself still grappling with life's frustrations and the lingering impact of past traumas.

The desire to escape led me to alcohol, creating a routine of putting on a smile at work, returning home, showering, consuming alcohol, and breaking down in tears, overwhelmed by the thought of continuing to live.

During these challenging times, I had a lifeline in the form of a friend named Harlene. When suicidal thoughts loomed, I would reach out to her, and she would urge me not to succumb to them.

One particularly dark night, I drank until I passed out while sitting naked in bed. Surprisingly, waking up the next morning, I realized I was still alive.

Regardless of the quantity of alcohol consumed, the problems persisted when I sobered up. The grip of the alcohol's influence seemed unrelenting, and I felt unable to break free from its hold.

It became a coping mechanism, a spirit that intertwined with my struggles. This dependence on alcohol was insidious, creating a false sense of relief that, ultimately, did not alleviate the underlying issues.

The various types of alcohol I turned to; whether Baileys, Wray and Nephew white rum and rum cream, red wine, special wines or cocktails like "sex on the beach"—each carried a distinct spirit, influencing my emotions and perceptions. I even made my own fruity alcohol drink.

Alcohol was Dominating My Life

Reflecting on the impact of different alcohols, I realized the danger in allowing this spirit to dominate one's life. Much like drugs, the spirit of alcohol can seize control, wreaking havoc on vital aspects of life such as health, relationships, and overall well-being.

The illusion that it is indispensable for functions like speech, sleep, or intimacy only adds to its destructive power.

Over time, I became aware that the spirit of alcohol, if left unchecked, could lead to addiction and the gradual deterioration of one's life. Its effects may not be immediately apparent, but with time, the toll on organs, relationships, and personal fulfillment becomes undeniable.

One day, my boyfriend shared something deeply distressing, triggering such intense anger that I impulsively grabbed a bottle of alcohol and consumed it rapidly, resulting in vomiting.

Fueled by the overwhelming emotions, I also took my

pornography DVD and shattered it, illustrating the extent of my frustration.

Prior to my second deployment to Iraq, my coworkers and I decided to celebrate at a bar. I ended up drinking excessively, and on the bus ride home from Manhattan to the Bronx, I repeatedly left messages on my boyfriend's voicemail.

The following day, he questioned me about the calls, and I was completely unaware of my actions.
The haziness of the night was apparent as I struggled to recall how I managed to walk from the bus stop to my apartment.

Recognizing the potential harm, I could inflict on myself, it became clear that it was time for me to stop drinking.

The incidents served as a wake-up call to address the destructive impact alcohol was having on my life and well-being.

It's a stark contrast between being under the influence of alcohol and the guidance of the Holy Spirit. Ephesians 5:18:

"And be not drunk with wine, wherein is excess; but be filled with the Spirit,"

This scripture text underscores the importance of avoiding excessive alcohol consumption, emphasizing the need to be filled with the Holy Spirit. Unlike the impairing effects of alcohol, the Holy Spirit provides a sound mind and prevents decisions that lead to regret or harm.

Reflecting on a night where I experienced a traumatic event, it became evident that the influence of red label wine weakened me, allowing the devil to gain control over my life.

The Holy Spirit had previously warned me, but I disregarded the guidance, resulting in disobedience to God and falling victim to deception.

This serves as a cautionary reminder not to be deceived into consuming alcohol that impairs judgment and opens the door to negative influences. Choosing the guidance of the Holy Spirit over the intoxicating effects of alcohol ensures a path of clarity, wisdom, and protection.

The Bible Even Speaks of the Consequences of Alcohol

Some adverse consequences of alcohol are documented in the Bible, as seen in Genesis 19:32, where Lot's daughters plotted to intoxicate their father, stating,

"Come, let us make our father drink wine, and we will lie with him, that we may preserve seed of our father."

They succeeded in making their father drink wine, leading to a situation where one of the daughters took advantage of his impaired state to engage in incestuous acts.

This instance illustrates the grave repercussions that can arise when alcohol is used to manipulate and facilitate immoral behavior. The consequences of such actions extended to a curse on Lot's daughters and their future generations.

In 1 Samuel 1:14-15, a separate incident involving Hannah and Eli unfolds. Eli mistakenly accused Hannah of being drunk when, in fact, she was fervently praying and pouring out her soul before the Lord.

"And Eli said unto her, How long wilt thou be drunken? put away thy wine from thee. And Hannah answered and said, No, my lord, I am a woman of a sorrowful spirit: I have drunk neither wine nor strong drink but have poured out my soul before the LORD."

This misinterpretation underscores the importance of not making assumptions based solely on external observations, as speaking to oneself is not necessarily indicative of alcohol influence.

These biblical narratives collectively emphasize the potential dangers and negative impacts associated with alcohol misuse, emphasizing the need for discernment, responsible behavior, and an understanding of the moral consequences that may follow.

Chapter Five

POISON

Lessons

I understand that consuming wine is acceptable, but with a sense of moderation.

In Mark 14:22-24, during the Last Supper, Jesus shared bread and wine with his disciples, symbolizing his body and blood in the New Testament.

"While they were eating, Jesus took bread, and when he had given thanks, he broke it and gave it to his disciples, saying, "Take it; this is my body." Then he took a cup, and when he had given thanks, he gave it to them, and they all drank from it. "This is my blood of the[a] covenant, which is poured out for many," he said to them."

This event underscores the ceremonial and symbolic use of wine in communion, rather than advocating for its consumption for the purpose of intoxication.

Furthermore, 1 Timothy 5:23 advises against drinking only water, suggesting the use of a small amount of wine for health reasons related to stomach issues and frequent illnesses.

"Stop drinking only water and use a little wine because

of your stomach and your frequent illnesses."

This passage implies that there may be occasions when consuming a moderate amount of wine could be beneficial in addressing certain health issues.

Moderation in Alcohol Consumption:

Try to avoid drinking alcohol, and if you choose to drink, do so responsibly without getting drunk.

Guarding Personal Information:

Refrain from sharing too many details about yourself with individuals you're not in a dating relationship with, as some may exploit this information to cause harm.

Discerning God's Voice:

Develop the ability to recognize God's voice so that when He speaks, you can discern His guidance.

Following God's Instructions:

Remember and adhere to the instructions given by God, which may include warnings against excessive alcohol consumption.

Limitations of Alcohol:

Acknowledge that alcohol doesn't solve problems; instead, it often exacerbates existing issues.

Seeking Support:

If struggling with alcohol consumption, seek help from friends or family to overcome challenges associated with drinking.

Recognizing the Negative Influence:

Understand that the spirit of alcohol is considered harmful and has the potential to negatively impact and ruin various aspects of your life.

Chapter Five

POISON

❖ Lord thank you for forgiving me for giving control to the spirit of the alcohol over my life.

❖ I renounce the relationship I have with the spirit of alcohol in the name of Jesus Christ.

❖ I lose myself from the spirit of alcohol in the name of Jesus Christ.

❖ I bind the spirit of alcohol in the name of Jesus Christ.

❖ I cast out the spirit of alcohol out of my body and life in the name of Jesus Christ.

❖ The spirit of alcohol will not return to my life nor follow me around in the name of Jesus Christ.

❖ I cancel the plan of the devil and enemies for me to get rape again in the name of Jesus Christ.

❖ I shall not reap what my ancestors has done to others in the name of Jesus.

❖ The spirit of God will lead and direct me wherever to go and when not to go and who to be close to in the name of Jesus.

❖ I pray that the spirit of alcoholism will not operate in your life in the name of Jesus.

❖ I surrender my body, soul and spirit to the Holy Spirit of God.

❖ Lord God give me justice for my rape in the name of Jesus Christ.

Reflections

Heavenly Father, I come before You with a humble heart, acknowledging my shortcomings and the times I've allowed the spirit of alcohol to take control of my life. I recognize the mistakes I've made and the consequences that have followed. Lord, I thank for Your Forgiveness and mercy.

Thank You, Father, for Your boundless love and forgiveness. I trust in Your mercy and believe that, through Your grace, I can overcome the challenges I face.

Chapter Six

THE CURSE

Why Does a little girl like older woman?

When I was younger, I noticed that little boys were interested in having girlfriends, and older men would sometimes stare at me, which left me feeling disgusted.

There was a time when my grandmother would attend a yearly Pentecostal Convention Service in a specific district, and I found myself drawn to it. Not for the service itself, but because there was a beautiful Christian lady I liked to see there. Although I couldn't understand why I was more interested in seeing her than the actual service.

I recall a similar experience in high school when we got a new female teacher, and I found myself infatuated with her. I expressed my feelings to her, and she kindly explained that she was not interested in girls, helping me understand that my feelings were not reciprocated.

Despite the awareness that my feelings weren't reciprocated, I continued to look at her and engage in conversations whenever I had the chance.

At the time, I didn't perceive it as wrong; in my mind, it was simply a matter of liking her.

The internal turmoil I was experiencing made it challenging to process what was happening, as I felt influenced by conflicting emotions driven by both the homosexual and lusting spirits.

Remarkably, I didn't experience shame for desiring her while being aware of her lack of interest. She continued to interact with me as usual.

It was an unusual circumstance since, generally, I didn't harbor romantic feelings for any other females.

Definitions

__Homosexuality__ is a <u>romantic</u> attraction, <u>sexual attraction</u>, or <u>sexual behavior</u> between members of the same <u>sex</u> or <u>gender.</u> People who identify as homosexual are attracted emotionally, romantically, and/or sexually to individuals of the same sex.

I had a friend whom people speculated was a lesbian, but I didn't mind because she was a great friend and a genuinely kind person. She treated me well and was always there for me, truly a friend sent by God. Other females were envious of our friendship.

I had an interest in her male friend who had feelings for me. However, she disapproved of my choice of clothing, particularly shirts that reached my bottom or short blouses exposing my belly. One day, she refused to walk with me due to my attire.

My mother, too, disapproved of such clothing choices. I enjoyed turning my pants into shorts, although I sometimes felt uncomfortable, anticipating judgment from others.

109

Despite spending a significant amount of time with my female friend, our relationship never ventured into the realm of romantic or sexual feelings.

Surprisingly, another female friend of mine, who was bisexual, mistakenly believed there was more between us. She refused to accept my assurance that there wasn't.

My Goal was to Show Women how to be Loved by a Man

Upon arriving in America and joining the US Army, I found that my feelings towards women began to grow. While back in Jamaica, there were only two individuals who sparked such emotions.

The dynamics changed in America, possibly influenced by the prevalent presence of the homosexual spirit in the environment.

The widespread acceptance of diverse sexual orientations contributed to a heightened awareness of these feelings, with a discernible energy around individuals with a homosexual orientation.

The challenges I faced in seeking love and validation from men, coupled with past hurts, seemed to pave the way for the awakening of the homosexual spirit within me.

In response, I found myself desiring love and connection with women, exploring relationships and connections with female friends.

I felt a preference for feminine women, as opposed to those with a more masculine appearance; referred to as 'butch.'

I identified with being a butch myself. My desire was to express love to a woman in a way that aligned with traditional masculine roles.

This period marked a significant shift in my understanding of love and relationships, influenced by both personal experiences and the cultural context of my new surroundings.

My Life was Changing.

My life was undergoing profound changes as I began to navigate the waters of bisexuality. I wasn't indiscriminately engaging with every woman I met.

I was aware of the societal and religious views against same-sex relationships, particularly in my homeland, Jamaica, where such relationships are frowned upon.

My conscience often wrestled with the feelings I harbored whenever I found myself attracted to another woman.

Emulating masculine traits, like grabbing the crotch of my pants and braiding my hair, became part of my expression of self, as did pursuing women in a manner typically associated with men.

Despite the freedom to live as I chose, I wasn't immune to external perceptions or attention from women I wasn't interested in. My preferences in women were as personal and specific as they were for men.

Straddling the boundaries of societal norms, I found a strange comfort, dwelling in the discomfort of my bisexuality.

During my initial deployment with the US Army in Kuwait, I took the bold step of trimming my hair into a men's style, and I instantly fell in love with the look.

This was a time of immense transition in my life, as I was becoming acquainted with lesbian couples and women, I found attractive, as well as women who reciprocated that attraction.

It caught me off guard when a woman I knew approached and kissed me.

It's simpler to deflect an unwanted advance from a man than from a woman you find attractive.

I had a particularly strong attraction to a close friend while overseas and asked her if she would consider a relationship with me. She was strikingly beautiful, but she gently turned me down, stating she was not interested in women.

I respected her decision, even though I broached the subject with her a second time. We remain friends to this day, both devoting ourselves to serving God.

After this deployment, I found myself spending more time with a female friend of mine and her two sisters.

We shared countless evenings filled with laughter and stories, creating a bond that was both profound and intimate. It was during this time that they revealed a secret: they harbored romantic feelings toward the same sex.

One sister was openly bisexual, a fact already known to us.

However, her two sisters' revelation was new. It made me realize how sexual orientation can be influenced by surroundings and company.

If constantly around someone with a homosexual orientation, the possibility of developing similar feelings or tendencies can't be entirely ruled out.

It doesn't necessarily mean one succumbs to these feelings, but the temptation could arise.

It might lead to a moment of vulnerability where one might consider acting upon these feelings, maybe through a kiss or an attempt at a sexual act.

This experience shed light on my understanding of human sexuality, reminding me how complex and fluid it can be.

During a particular training period in the military, I noticed that one instructor seemed to single me out consistently. I could not understand her intentions until the day she invited me to her office for a conversation.

During this unexpected meeting, we shared a kiss, and it became clear that she was attracted to me - an attraction that was apparent to our classmates.

I expressed to her my commitment to my training, but it was impossible to deny the burgeoning sexual tension between us, given that she was my instructor.

We decided to postpone any further involvement until after my graduation.

Upon completing my training, we had another conversation where I informed her about my boyfriend. I suggested the idea of a threesome, considering my boyfriend was aware of my interest in women and had expressed a similar desire. However, she did not share our sentiments.

This relationship with my instructor was my only serious and long-term relationship with a woman. I played the more masculine role, yet she insisted on paying for our outings, which was contrary to the conventional norms and hence, confusing. She even harbored dreams of marriage and moving to Hawaii.

Despite these feelings, I was constantly plagued by guilt, knowing that being with her felt wrong. I was certain that God and my family would disapprove and be upset with me. I introduce her to my one of my sisters as a friend.

No One Really Knew Me

The turmoil within me was a secret, a heavy burden that I bore alone.

Whether I was with my boyfriend or my girlfriend, a phone call from the other would send me whispering into the receiver, trying to hide the fact that I was with someone else.

My life felt like a twisted game, and I grew weary of it.

One day, as I was with my girlfriend and on the phone with my boyfriend, both of them angrily demanded my full attention. I remember declaring that I couldn't tolerate this life anymore.

There were also nights when my girlfriend, got drunk and overwhelmed, would call me, pleading to get married. She'd question why I wouldn't leave my boyfriend and marry her instead.

The cycle would repeat itself when I embarked on military training. She'd get drunk again, drive to my hotel unannounced, and frustrate me. This unending cycle of emotional turbulence and strain was exhausting and left me questioning the life I had chosen.

My phone buzzed, it was her, saying she was outside, the slurred words revealing her heavy intoxication. I was seized with fear and anger as I realized she could have crashed the truck during her journey from Fort Dix, New Jersey to Brooklyn.

My boyfriend had left my hotel just a few hours earlier. I cried out, "Oh no! This is not what God wants from me." That was the moment I decided to end our relationship. I chose to be with a man, refusing to defy God's will any further.

As a backslider, I felt that God was calling me back and I was ready to answer that call. My time with women had ended.

I was Being Deployed

Fate had other plans.

As I was preparing for deployment, she showed up uninvited at my unit barracks. I was in a unit I never wanted to be in; ironically, it included other lesbians. The units were a hotbed of drama, and despite my clear stand about having a boyfriend and not being interested in anyone, rumors started swirling.

Someone falsely claimed I was sleeping with a female soldier, which was impossible given I was spending my nights with my boyfriend. I was ensnared in a web of lies and deceit, an unfortunate situation that I had not envisaged.

Some females can be cruel when they can't have you. My boyfriend advised me to tell my ex-girlfriend not to come to our barracks. During a cookout, she unexpectedly showed up on her motorcycle, another lesbian in my unit had invited her.

I was shocked and had to explain to my boyfriend that I didn't invite her or know she was coming.

It's funny how, after my overseas tour in 2009, I tried to reach out to her to apologize for how I treated her. However, she expressed anger and never followed through on meeting and talking. I had already apologized, so I was at peace.

Since that relationship, I have not been with another woman.

In 2012, after becoming saved, I reached out to God to help me change internally and be delivered from the spirit of homosexuality.

I began avoiding physical contact with females, unless it was necessary for a testimony.

I would share with the church to pray for homosexual individuals, as they might have been molested, seeking love, or influenced by a spirit.

There are various reasons why someone might become

homosexual. Praying for them and asking God for deliverance from that spirit is crucial. That's how I became free from desiring women and only desiring a man, as God spoke in Genesis 3:16:

"Unto the woman he said... and thy desire shall be to thy husband, and he shall rule over thee."

The devil and his demons would get upset and occasionally send a woman in my dreams or tempt me in real life.

Over the years, I've learned that;

Forgiveness Is The Key To Finding Inner Peace

I have forgiven those who hurt me, and I have sought forgiveness from those whom I've hurt. I've made a conscious effort to live a life that aligns with my beliefs and values. I've also learned that it's essential to have a support system during this journey of change.

I've also found solace and strength in my faith and in my church community, who have provided me with guidance and love.

I believe God has a plan for each one of us, and my journey has led me to find my true self.

Each day presents its challenges, but each day also brings me closer to living the life I've always desired.

I share my story in hopes that it will inspire others who might be struggling with their sexuality or identity, and to let them know they are not alone.

I'm Married Now

In 2017, I had just started a new job. A woman of God whom I had admired informed me that a church brother of hers from Jamaica would contact me via Facebook Messenger.

I explained to Minister Kelly that I wasn't currently open to dating and was attending Bible study at the time, suggesting we speak the next day.

After speaking over the phone, we agreed to courtship after a few weeks. He won me over with his deep understanding of the word of God. Eventually, we got married in 2018.

Navigating these encounters proved challenging, as feelings of confusion and temptation arose.

A coworker and friend of mine began to develop feelings for me. One day she openly propositioned me.

Despite the shock of her overture, I firmly declined, asserting that I was both committed to my husband and to my service to God.

Similarly, clients from my previous job who identified as homosexual made advances towards me.

Each time, I rejected their advances, choosing to honor my faith and my marriage vows.

In a separate incident, another female friend persistently complimented my physical appearance, which initially seemed harmless. However, her actions intensified over time and culminated in a moment when, after hugging me and kissing my cheek, I was struck by the realization that she might harbor feelings for me.

The thought crossed my mind that this could be a ploy by the devil to tempt me, but I remained unmoved. Instead, I chose to handle the situation with care. I limited my interactions by being careful what I said and how I acted around her.

In hindsight, I remember having an uneasy feeling about this friend, a feeling that left me wondering if the problem lay with me. Eventually, it dawned on me that perhaps God was signaling that something was awry.

Heeding this intuition, I gradually reduced our conversations, and over time, God brought an end to that relationship.

Reject those feelings of same-sex relations

"When you find yourself attracted to the scent of someone of the same sex, consciously acknowledge and resist these feelings, pray and seek the Holy Spirit for strength to turn away."

If you find comfort in the company of a person of the same sex, to the extent that you feel jealousy when they interact with others, or a lack of interest in the opposite sex, it's important to acknowledge these feelings and call out to Jesus for help.

The same applies if you find yourself desiring physical contact with someone of the same sex. If you're feeling at ease when someone of the same sex touches you, or are looking forward to such encounters, especially if it involves intimate touch, consciously resist these feelings and seek spiritual support.

If you notice a person who identifies as homosexual showing interest in you, and you reciprocate with smiles or prolonged eye contact, they may get the wrong impression. Be cautious and mindful of your actions and interactions.

Navigating conversations about same-sex attractions can be complex, particularly if they lead to discussions about personal experiences or hypothetical scenarios. It's crucial to approach these talks with caution, as they may signify an individual's attempt to gauge your views or experiences concerning same- sex relationships.

If you find yourself in such a situation, it's advisable not to entertain the discussion, as it may invite unwanted speculation or misunderstandings.

As believers, we should recall Romans 1:27-28, which states,

"And likewise, also the men, leaving the natural use of the woman, burned in their lust one toward another; men with men working that which is unseemly, and receiving in themselves that recompense of their error which was meet. And even as they did not like to retain God in their knowledge, God gave them over to a reprobate mind, to do those things which are not convenient."

Therefore, it is essential to steer clear of conversations that might steer us away from the teachings of Scripture.

Human Relationships and Sexuality

In my personal view, consistently disregarding the belief that men should not be with other men or women with other women could lead to divine consequences: you will suffer the consequences of disobeying God's law.

In addition, there is no way that two men or two women can have a child together.

This viewpoint is often underscored by the biological reality that same-sex couples cannot naturally conceive children together.

Therefore, God's command in Genesis 1:28:

"Be fruitful, and multiply, and replenish the earth,"

cannot be adhered to nor fulfilled.

Indeed, there have been instances where individuals who identify as women, yet were biologically born male, have impregnated individuals who identify as men, but were biologically born female.

This occurs because their original reproductive organs were not altered, despite their change in gender identity and physical appearance.

God designed female bodies to bear children, receiving the male partner's seed for reproduction. Although men can provide the seed, they are not physically equipped to carry a child.

From what I have witnessed and learned; conflicts may occur in any relationship, more so in homosexual relationships. Fighting spirits and financial instability is more dominant in same sex relationships because these issues cross the boundaries of sexual orientation.

When they have a fight, and the man even if he identifies himself as a woman will get in trouble for hitting the women partner. A man is not supposed to hit a woman.

These attacks are directly from evil spirits because of the couples disobeying God and doing things contrary to His Word.

I have seen and experienced many of these arguments which were so unnecessary.

Some of them led to the other having a mental breakdown.

Financially they struggle and suffer to find stability and peace in their lives.

These traumas I mention don't happen to everyone. These experiences and insights are not representative of the entire LGBTQ+ community but are drawn from a small number of individuals I've interacted with, and revelations granted through the Holy Spirit.

I must say that there are some homosexual relationships which are good and have no physical problem but spiritual they are affected. Regardless of that it still isn't right according to God.

Regardless of the gender they identify themselves by; it's important that we understand the diversity of human relationships and identities, so we know what to pray for and set those in bondage free.

Remember, God knew us before He formed us in our mother's womb. He knew that each one of us navigates a different path in life, filled with unique experiences and lessons, but not homosexuality.

It's not our role to pass judgment on these journeys but to extend empathy, support, and love. Pray for them and not judge them.

"Do not judge, or you too will be judged. For in the same way, you judge others, you will be judged, and with the measure you use, it will be measured to you." (Matthew 7:1-2)

I'm Still Ignorant in Some Matters

One aspect I am ignorant of pertains to the physical aspects of same-sex relationships, particularly where artificial implements such as fake male sex organ are involved. Rather than doing it the natural way; they use synthetic tools for penetration which takes away from the experience of feeling the real thing.

The feeling of warmness from the sexual organs between and man and woman touching each other is something you cannot replicate.

The sensation of natural intimacy is absent, replaced by a manufactured experience that lacks warmth, connection, and emotional bonding.

Children Struggles

The devil as gone so far with his cruelty that he has the young children confuse about their identity. Boys want to be girls and girls want to be boys. The worst thing is that they are teaching the children in school what it is like to be gay and that they should express their feelings.

The spirit of homosexuality has caught the children from they were young and parents and guardians are giving into it. Remember what happen to me.

GENDER IDENTITY CHECKLIST

Exploring one's sexual orientation is a personal and individual journey. It can be helpful to reflect on your feelings, experiences, and attractions.

Questions To Ask Yourself

- Who am I emotionally and romantically attracted to?

- Who do I fantasize about or have crushes on?

- Do I find myself being attracted to people of the same sex?

- How do I feel about the idea of being in a same-sex relationship?

- Are there any patterns or trends in my past relationships or attractions?

- How do I feel when I see or think about same-sex couples or LGBTQ+ representation?

- Have I ever had any same-sex experiences or attractions?

- Do I feel like I'm homosexual?

- Am I comfortable being a homosexual?

- What made me become a homosexual?

Remember, it's important to take your time, be honest with yourself, and seek support if needed.

Chapter Six

THE CURSE

Lessons

- Molestation and incest open up your spirit to other spirits such as lust, seduction, homosexuality, spirit husband or wife and many other evil spirits.

- You can be possessed by the spirit of homosexuality though many ways such as sexual promiscuity, pornography, masturbation, at birth, through generational curses, blood line, cults, covenants and witchcraft.

- God is against homosexuality.

- God always speaks to us about our sin.

- You need deliverance from the spirit for homosexuality and the spirit that opens you up to homosexuality.

- A homosexual lifestyle brings destruction and pain more than a normal heterosexual relationship.

- If you are a homosexual God loves you. Check your life and see how much God has been reaching out to you.

- Fight the urge to want to experience what it is like to be with the same sex, sexually.

- Resist the spirit of homosexuality, masturbation and pornography.

- When you have realized that some of the same sex body scent is getting you aroused reject that feeling in the name of Jesus.

- If you notice a strong desire to be around individuals of the same sex, find comfort in their presence, have an indifference towards the opposite sex, or jealousy when the person you're drawn to is with someone else, it may mean you have the spirit of homosexuality.

  In such cases, lean on your faith in Jesus. For instance, you may choose to pray or ask someone you can trust to pray for you.

  Remember, your feelings are a part of you, and understanding them is the first step towards self-acceptance. If you're experiencing confusion or distress, consider seeking support from understanding loved ones or professional counselors.

- If you enjoy someone that is the same sex touching you and you touching them and you can't wait for them to touch you again and if they touch your private and you don't mind, reject that feeling in the name of Jesus.

- If you know that someone is homosexual and they are looking at you and you keep staring and giving a smile or good eye, contact they will assume you are interested in them.

- If someone initiates a conversation about being intimate with a person of the same sex or expresses interest in trying it, it is important to be cautious.

  Engaging in such discussions may invite unwanted energy or influence.

  It is advisable to refrain from entertaining these conversations, as they may attract a homosexual spirit.

  Focus on maintaining healthy boundaries and redirecting the conversation if necessary.

Chapter Six

THE CURSE

- ❖ Lord help me not to be confuse about my identity.

- ❖ Lord help me and deliver me from the spirit that cause me to become a homosexual.

- ❖ Lord, thank you for forgiving me for being with the same sex and going against your word.

- ❖ Holy Spirit I'm sorry for defiling Your body.

- ❖ I renounce the relationship I have with the homosexual spirit, in the name of Jesus Christ.

- ❖ I command the homosexual spirit to loose me in the name of Jesus Christ

- ❖ I bind you up homosexual spirit in the name of Jesus Christ.

- ❖ I send you, homosexual spirit out of my body and never

return to my life again, in the name of Jesus Christ.

❖ Every spirit that came in my life through the spirit of homosexual I command you all (say the names) to go, in the name of Jesus.

❖ Father God, please cleanse me with the blood of Jesus, in the name of Jesus Christ.

❖ Lord God, please send the right opposite sex partner You have for me, in the name of Jesus Christ.

Reflections

Dear Heavenly Father,

I come before you in humility, thanking for your mercy and guidance. I confess my actions and acknowledge that they may not align with Your divine principles.

Lord, I ask for Your help and deliverance from the spirit that may lead me towards homosexuality. I thank you for Your forgiveness for my past actions. I am ready to renounce any relationship that I may have with a spirit that encourages homosexuality. I pray this in the powerful and redemptive name of Jesus Christ. Amen.

Chapter Seven

MY TORTURE

Masturbation is the sexual stimulation of one's own genitals for sexual arousal or other sexual pleasure, usually to the point of orgasm.

Lying in bed one night and decided to touch myself. I continued and something happened. It felt good. I didn't know what it was called, but I tried it a few more times.

Was it something natural and against God?

I didn't know whether it was or not. I have never heard anyone talk about it before.

As I got older and became more sexually active, I began this act, more and more.

I begin watching porn and learned that what I was doing was referred to as masturbation. To help me masturbate I would watch a video of my boyfriend.

Masturbation became a norm for me. Sometimes I would please myself while doing a video call, during phone sex or with my girlfriend or boyfriend. I was fascinated and addicted to masturbation.

I went to the sex toy store and bought different types of sex toys to please myself. I would google the toys.

I remember the first sex toy was from a boyfriend I had.

We were walking in the Village in Manhattan, and I saw one named, 'the rabbit.' I asked my boyfriend for it and he bought it for me. I had seen the toys in porn movies and was intrigued.

That started my frequent shopping spree on sex toys. My body was calling for me to masturbate. It's like I couldn't control myself. It seems the spirit of masturbation took me over.

Yes, the spirit of masturbation, it took me over.

It got so bad that I bought a lipstick vibrator toy to carry in my purse. I would be at work and get the urge to masturbate. I would get up, take a break just so I could go do it.

It felt like I was being turned on by my own body.

Sounds crazy right?

I had to wear certain underwear to help me not feel my own vagina being turned on. Certain materials would make me get aroused.

At times I felt like I was going crazy.

Masturbation is a Wicked Tormenting Spirit

My skin or some place on my body would start itching, causing me to masturbate. It got to the point where I begin masturbating; morning, afternoon, night. I mean, anytime.

I could masturbate in a way that no one was aware of what I was

135

doing.

I knew something was wrong with me. Especially when I masturbated until my clitoris was tender and I still didn't stop. I had to use Vaseline to help me and even then, I still did it.

Oh, that wicked spirit was tormenting me.

I would buy a new sex toy before the week was over and then throw it away when the Holy Spirit convicted me. I was a backslider, but the Holy Spirit still reprimanded me. The Holy Spirit never stopped warning me when I was doing something wrong. I would repent and say, "I'm sorry, Lord."

Guess what? I went back the very next week and got another one.

Even if I wasn't buying, I found the store and went eye shopping. I even found websites that sell the toys. I wasted so much money on sex toy.

The toys were good when I was away from my boyfriend and even used the toys during our sexual act. People say toys spice up the relationship, but it actually takes away the pleasure of your partner pleasing you and detracts you from the joy derived from your partner's affection.

Later you start to rely on the toy instead of your partner.

They served as a satisfactory substitute during my boyfriend's absence. Over time, you may find yourself relying more on the toy for your pleasure than your partner. I had my experience when I was serving in Iraq and away from my boyfriend.

I never liked the strap-on male sex organ because I love the real one. Toys were just for when I was alone or wanted to spice up my sex life with my boyfriend.

What really doesn't make any sense is when the female is with another female, and they use this strap-on male sex organ. What is the sense of leaving a man to be with a woman and then go buy a false male sex organ to have sex with a woman? You may as well stay with the man. It's a false male sex organ penetrating the woman, not a real one.

Toys were not good yet; they were appealing to anyone who claimed to be a freak or homosexual. Many homosexuals use sex toys because they have strayed away from the natural way of sex that God made.

Lord, Help me with the Things I cannot Change.

Using the sex toy to masturbate made it easier for me because the vibration makes me have an orgasm faster.

It's faster than a man so, hey, why not use it?

However, it pulls you away from your man and allows a sex demon to take over. You start to fantasize about your man making love to you or doing sexual things to you, while you use your toy.

Now that opens up a door to a sex demon can be a male (incubus) or female (succubus) sex demon. Each time you use it alone or with your man, you are having sex with that demon.

In your mind; at that time; it would seem like it's your man you are having sex, but it is male or female sex demon you got from using the sex toy. These sex toys like the bullet, beads or others will let you want to try having anal sex. God is against all of this.

I became a Christian and still masturbated.

That spirt of masturbation was still living in me.

I thought that once I got saved all freaky sexual things I used to do would go and I would be free.

But no.
It took a while because I had to pray especially for this masturbation spirit to let me go as I renounced the relationship with it.

This spirit was deeply ingrained in me, starting from my teenage years and continuing into adulthood. It was a long- lasting connection, almost like a marriage.

Disposing of the sex toy was pretty easy, yet I found myself drawn to a vibrating massager. The nature of addiction is such that it can coax you into finding alternative ways to satisfy those nasty desires.

Even though I didn't do it as much as I did before giving my life to the Lord and becoming a Christian, the struggle was real.

I sought the Lord's help, frequently praying to overcome the spirit of masturbation. It became evident that resisting these urges was a battle I couldn't fight alone, and I continually asked

God for strength.

Thank God for Deliverance

God delivered me from the spirit of masturbation, and although I still have moments where I must resist the urge, I find pleasure in my husband rather than resorting to my own hand or a toy.

Each person and marriage are different. Different people and marriages possess unique characteristics.

Incorporating masturbation and the use of sex toys introduce a foreign element into your life and marriage. The practices of using sex toys and masturbation invite a spirit to take on the form of the person you are fantasizing about having sex with.

Whenever your partner is unavailable, both husband and wife may resort to masturbation or seek a toy for self-pleasure.

It's a fact that some men explore alternative methods when their wives are not accessible. This could involve using their fingers for self-pleasure or to masturbation.

Consequently, this could lead to confusion where a man unexpectedly finds himself drawn to other men and engage in intimate relations with them.

This creates a pathway to men masturbating with other men and doing unnatural things. Women too can find comfort in other women and play sexual games with each other leading to masturbation.

You see, one freaky act leads to another freaky act then your life is in turmoil.

Don't let people fool you about how masturbation is healthy for you. That is the way for the devil to deceive us to please ourselves and have the sex demon's incubus and succubus molesting you.

Sex toys brings a quick pleasure, but receiving pleasure from your partner is longer and connects you to him or her.

Your partner playing with you is a whole different ballgame. This is a natural act because you are both pleasing one other and enjoying the sensation in your bodies.

Don't let the devil fool you that when you away from each other to masturbate over the video call or phone.

You in turn can become addicted to masturbation and quick to please yourself rather than waiting for your partner to pleasure you. Be mindful if you decide to try doing it.

Masturbation can influence you to let anyone touch you just so you can receive pleasure.

Masturbation Can Cost You Your Life

I remember a time where I was being stalked by a man. That person would call my phone and I could tell by the sounds he was making that he was masturbating as he listened to my voice. I reported him to the police.

Another time I was dating someone from an online dating app

and the man would masturbate over the phone and make sounds.

The day we met in person he told me how he would get off by hearing my voice. I said, "really?" and he did it right there in front of me.

He was addicted to masturbation, and it did not matter to him where or when he would do it.

I would enjoy watching someone doing it; especially if it was my boyfriend.

I had to stop.

God was the solution for me stop.

Masturbation can lead to many sinful acts and evil spirits taking over our lives.

There are not many scriptures about it so people think it is good to do, but it is not.

Please don't let the devil fool you.

Chapter Seven

MY TORTURE

<u>Lessons</u>

- Masturbation leads to fornication and to addiction to pornography

- Masturbation leads to adultery, someone masturbating for you and an inability to resist. It can lead to cheating on your partner.

- Masturbation leads to perverted acts such as a man masturbating to a child or women in public.

- Masturbation causes us to have a spirit husband or wife.

- Masturbation can cause you to become a prostitute because you find multiple partners to ensure you always get your sexual desire fulfilled.

- Masturbation leads you to be addicted to it like a drug.

- Masturbation can lead to isolation because you rather isolate yourself to continuously pleasure yourself than be with people

- Masturbation can lead to anger because when you have the urge to do it and someone is hindering you, you will tend to get angry at that person.

- Masturbation can lead to depression because if you are deprived of it, you can get depressed from not doing it.

Chapter Seven

MY TORTURE

❖ Lord thank you for forgiving me for masturbating to please my flesh.

❖ Lord please don't let my life be ruined by the spirit of masturbation.

❖ Lord grant me the strength to overcome my desire to masturbate in Jesus Name.

❖ I renounce the relationship I have with the spirit of masturbation in the name of Jesus Christ.

❖ I command the masturbation spirit to loose me in the name of Jesus Christ.

❖ I bind you up masturbation spirit in the name of Jesus Christ.

❖ I send you masturbation spirit out of me and never return

to my life again in the name of Jesus Christ.

❖ Lord let me see Your glory in my life and not return to the destructive habit of masturbation in the name of Jesus Christ.

I confess that I have allowed my desires to lead me astray, to commit adultery in my heart, to objectify others, and to develop a spirit spouse. The lust of my flesh has driven me to the point where I fear I may lose sight of the sanctity and exclusivity of a romantic relationship.

I acknowledge that these acts have led me down a path that is not of Your design, causing me to veer from the purpose You have set for me.

I understand now that my actions may push me to depths I never intended to reach, such as engaging in illicit acts in public or even turning to prostitution to satiate my ever- growing desires. Please guide me, Lord, in this journey towards freedom and healing. I trust in Your love and your power to deliver me from this bondage. In Jesus' name, I pray. Amen

.

Reflections

Dear Heavenly Father, I come to you in humility and recognition of my weakness, acknowledging that I was bound by the chains of self-pleasure.

Thank you for Your forgiveness, cleansing my heart and my mind from this addiction, from the longing that has taken hold of me. I believe that through Your mercy and grace, I can overcome this.

Thank you for the strength to resist these unholy desires, to maintain purity in my thoughts and actions.

Chapter Eight

THE ADDICTION

The newest technique the devil created is to have more pornography accessed through video chat on your computer and phone and social media. Years ago, you would have to buy porn DVDs or rent the video or go to a porn shop to watch it and watch someone having sex live or masturbate live.

The devil has made this so easy for those who are addicted to pornography or those who want to masturbate or learn how to use sex toys. It has been made more convenient for those who are learning how to have sex for the first time.

Even for those who are learning how to have orgies or to have sex with the same sex. It is teaching individuals how to spice up the bedroom.

Little did I know it was another trap and way for a different evil spirit to ruin my life.

Pornography (colloquially known as **porn** or **porno**) has been defined as <u>sexual subject</u> material "such as a picture, video, or text," that is considered <u>sexually arousing.</u>

During my time in high school, I would rent video cassette porn movies. I would watch it in the video shop and then trade it out for a new video.

There was a time when I took it to a place I was staying and watch it. It was nothing to me. No more than watching a movie and seeing how men and women would have sex.

It was fascinating to me how these men's sex organ was so long and women would cry from the pain but it did not deter them from having sex with them. I thought I was learning what it was like to have sex and what to do.

When I came to America and it was easier for me to get access to pornography. I was finding everything I needed to feed my inner secret desires and the evil spirits that possessed me.

I would see the porn shops view the previews of porn movies and buy different DVDs. I had my DVD player and could watch it anytime I wanted to.

I had to hide my DVD so that no one could find it. The last porn DVD I had; I broke it out of anger after an argument with my boyfriend. I don't know why I broke it when I needed it.

I became frustrated over not having the DVD because I used it as a means to help me to masturbate.

I decided to search the web for free porn sites. I didn't want to buy the porn on the cable channel. I found few sites and paid for them so I can watch porn to entertain myself and fulfill my nasty desire. It was pretty difficult finding free porn websites.

After searching for a while, I found one and I became more addicted to porn.

I was so far gone in watching them and using them to masturbate that it caused me to use the sex toys even more and desire sex beyond my comprehension. I didn't have to be pleased; I just enjoyed the act.

My past molestations and rapes turned me into a monster, I became a person without feeling who just wanted to quench the sexual desire. These spirits were controlling me and I was out of order. I was forced to do things I didn't want to do.

Watching porn and masturbating was my way of taking control of my sex life and doing what I wanted to do.

I watched the porn website everyday like it was a regular movie channel. There were so many different types of porn that I never knew existed. It was like a world of its own and it has everything someone might need.

In my relationship my boyfriend and I watched porn, after I while I suggest that we don't watch and just focus on each other, it was too much for me.

How was this possible that some of sexual acts were so disgusting and against natural sex acts being done on the website?

Someone who found the site didn't have to worry about paying for it was free. You would be drawn to see sexual acts that left you wondering if you should try them.

I was like. 'Is this for real?'

Real talk.

Thank God that I wasn't that crazy or addicted to these acts' sexual acts to the point that I was eager to try them. I knew God and he made sure I didn't indulge in certain things even though I had strayed far away from Him.

Now there are movies that are called 'soft porn.' They call it soft porn because it's not as raw as the hard pornography movies so, be mindful.

The devil again is very deceiving and if you won't search for porn, he will entice you watch a love move and then in the middle of the movie; a raw sex scene come in.

By then, you have already begun to enjoy the movie and you want to watch it to see how it ends. This has happened to me a few times and I had to fight the urge as a Child of God not to continue watch the movie.

Soft or hard pornography will lead you to try unnatural sexual acts with yourself and others. I will not go into detail.

I do want to warn you that; if you are watching porn please stop and ask the Holy Spirit for forgiveness.

Submit yourselves therefore to God. Resist the devil, and he will flee from you." James 4 :7 KJV.

When the temptation comes for you to watch porn resist it and it will go away. You can pray, sing or find something else to do to get rid of the urge. Continuous ask God to help you in your weak time. He will never leave you nor forsake you ("Be strong and of a good courage, fear not, nor be afraid of them: for the LORD thy God, he it is that doth go with thee; he will not fail thee, nor forsake thee." Deuteronomy 31:6 KJV)

He promises to deliver you out of temptation ("And lead us not into temptation, but deliver us from evil: Matthew 6:13 KJV

Chapter Eight

THE ADDICTION

Lessons

- ❖ Beware of when you are getting too attached to something and you can't stay away.
- ❖ Beware of what you spend too much money or even your last dollar or borrow money to quench your desire.

- ❖ Check if you rather do a certain activity for hours than spend time with love ones even.

- ❖ Don't let sex toys take over your intimate relationship and you can't do without it or have sex without them.

- ❖ Beware when your partner always wanting to use sex toys on you to stimulate you instead of doing their self.

- ❖ Don't let sex movies stimulate you so that you can have sex it will lead to addiction and you rely on the sex movie every time it is time for sex.

- ❖ You can become possessed or influenced by the sexual perversion spirit to try various nasty sexual acts from pornography so, STAY AWAY.

- ❖ Get help if you are addicted to porn and ask God to set you free from that spirit.

Chapter Eight

'THE ADDICTION'

❖ Lord God thank you for forgiving me for watching pornography or for the times I did in my life in the name of Jesus.

❖ Lord, please close the door of pornography in my life in the name of Jesus.

❖ Lord, I scatter every device or weapon use to let me watch pornography in the name of Jesus Christ.

❖ Separate me oh Lord from people or mediums and spirits that led me to pornography in the name of Jesus Christ.

❖ Let me be more like you oh Lord and help me to live a righteous life in the name of Jesus Christ.

❖ I renounce the relationship I have with you spirit of pornography in the name of Jesus Christ.

❖ I bind up you spirit of pornography in the name of Jesus Christ.

❖ I commanded you spirit of pornography to loose me in the name of Jesus Christ.

- ❖ I send you spirit of pornography to the pit of hell and never to return back to my life in the name of Jesus Christ.
- ❖ Lord, I thank you in the name of Jesus Christ for setting me from free from the bondage of the spirit of pornography.

I pray for strength, Lord. Your promise in Deuteronomy 31:6 reassures me that you go with me, that I need not fear, for You will neither fail nor forsake me. In moments of weakness, grant me courage and resilience to resist the devil, knowing that as I draw closer to You, the temptations will flee.

I lift up the struggle against the specific temptation to watch pornography. Fill my heart and mind with pure thoughts, and when the urge arises, guide me to pray, to sing praises to Your name, or to find constructive and uplifting activities that will redirect my focus.

Lord, I continuously ask for Your help in my weak times. Be my refuge and strength. Your promise to deliver us from temptation, as stated in Matthew 6:13, is my hope. I trust in Your faithfulness and ask for the grace to overcome these challenges. In Jesus' name, amen.

Reflections

Heavenly Father,

I come before you, acknowledging your sovereignty and power. Your word in James 4:7 reminds me to submit myself to You and resist the temptations that seek to pull me away from Your path. Lord, I recognize the struggle and the battles within, especially when faced with the temptation to watch things that dishonor You.

Thank you, Lord, for your unfailing love and constant presence, Your Spirit that guides me, empowers me, and leads me on the path of righteousness

Chapter Nine

MY FLESH

Lust intense sexual desire or appetite

- I see you and I want you.
- I desire you and I fantasize what it would be like to have you.

I fought this feeling every day and it was a struggle. Looking for that gorgeous perfect man that never existed. I wanted to be pleased, but love and lust were problems.

I lusted for men in suits. There was something about a man in a nice suit, business and church suit, army uniform and looking neat and well dress. I don't touch them or say I want them. I wasn't going to let myself be downgraded by sleeping around with men.

One time I thought handsome good-looking men were good, but then it was a lie. I dated someone who wasn't too good looking and I realized it's the same dirty character.

Looks don't make you a good person. It's the good character you have. You can be good-looking or ugly and if you character is nasty then you will be ugly or uglier. A man dressing in a suit or uniform doesn't mean that he has a good heart.

And rend your heart, and not your garments. (Joel 2:13)

The word of God says, 'rend your heart and not the clothes look, but the heart is deceiving.' I have learned my lessons.

Now it doesn't matter to me if you have a shabby or good-looking suit or uniform on. Just like you see someone with a good-looking body, but that's all that person might have and nothing else.

The Bible speaks about the lust of the eyes and I was lusting with my eyes

For all that is in the world, the lust of the flesh, and the lust of the eyes, and the pride of life, is not of the Father, but is of the world". (1 John 2:16)

We have to try the heart of a man and not his sexual organs and good looks.

Going to church I saw many men well dressed. They looked very good in their suits as they preached the Word of God. Then, right after service they come to me saying they want to get together.

Are you kidding me?

You just finished preaching.

I didn't know at the time that the devil goes to church too.

God's Word in Job 1:6 reminds us that satan went into the presence of God:

Now there was a day when the sons of God came to present

themselves before the LORD, and Satan came also among them.

The devil was in church and was tempting men and women to lust in service.

As a teenager; I was shocked when the pastor approached me after church service and started talking about getting to know me.

Ever since then I said to myself; 'Oh, so they wear suits, but pretending to be holier than thou.'

Sad to say, that is when I started testing Christian men to see if they were faithful to God or to their wives. I used words to test them.

Oh no! I didn't promise them any sex.

No! No!

I didn't go around sleeping with them. I would notice how much a man would be lusting after me and the things he does to get my attention or words he told me.

After few conversations I would ask them; 'So, you want to have sex with me?

The answer would be, 'Yes, if you would.'

I would say, 'No, plus you are a Christian or a married man.

How can you be a Christian and say you living by the word of God and sleeping around with females?

That is wrong.

You are fornicating if you are not married and committing adultery; if you are married.'

I was so disappointed in a lot of Christian men, leaders and non-leaders who were pretending to be serving God yet, pursuing get young ladies in church.

Another thing I learned, years after is that these men were struggling with lust as I was. They couldn't control their self without the help of God.

We lust after the opposite sex because we like what we see.

Jesus said:

> *"But I say unto you, That whosoever looketh on a woman to lust after her hath committed adultery with her already in his heart (Matthew 5:28)."*

When you lust you are thinking of what you like about the person sexually and what you want to do. That's when the deep hunger for the person begins and one would do anything to satisfy that desire. Once it's satisfied that one time or after many times, you don't want the person anymore.

Then it becomes a problem.

The person will feel like they have been rejected and the other who has satisfied their longing for the other person is now happy. Demons, it appears have possessed both persons through the sexual acts and their lives are damaged both; physically and spiritually.

I wasn't going to be the one God was going to punish for dating a man in Church.

One time there was this nice virgin Christian young man a Pastor's son. We like each other, but I was a backslider. One day he asked if I could have sex with him and I told him, "no."

I suggested that he save himself for his wife and that I am not going to be responsible for taking him out of church.

He understood and we still remain friends. He had a desire, but I wasn't going to be the one to fulfill it.

I was involved with a married man, as you read earlier in the book. It wasn't my intention, and it happened. At the time, I believed it was acceptable because his wife was in another country and he pursued me.

My lust got the better of me and I got involved with another married man after I joined the army and it ended with us just being friends before we had sexual intercourse.

I remember one weekend I went to the Army BDU club and was dancing, wining, shaking my body and saw this security guard watching me. I started to tease him with dance moves. My friends and I spoke to him before we left the club.

To my surprise when I got to my class Monday morning it was security who was my instructor. I laughed for even though I was in my uniform and not civilian clothes he recognizes me and made a joke.

After this last experience I realized that being with a married man is wrong. I planned to be married one day and I didn't want my husband to cheat on me.

The spirit of lust didn't care that the man was married.

I desired a committed relationship, and that's when I recognized the wrongdoing in my actions. I haven't dated a married man since, at least to my knowledge, unless the man concealed that he was married.

Wait, I was browsing a dating website and found someone I was interested in. However, when I conducted a background check, I discovered that he was married. He claimed they didn't live together, but I chose to end that dating situation.

Despite engaging in inappropriate behavior, I recalled the teachings of God and desired to please Him. However, my human desires were in conflict with my spiritual intentions. I seemed to be under the control of this spirit of lust and other spirits.

However, my fear of potential infidelity and the prospect of becoming a stepmother, given my youth, made me uneasy.

I sought God's forgiveness for dating these two married men and prayed not to encounter such situations in my future marriage. I was determined not to repeat this mistake, mindful of the biblical principle from Galatians 6:7 –

"Be not deceived; God is not mocked: for whatsoever a man soweth, that shall he also reap."

Recognizing the impact of my actions, I worked diligently to make sound decisions and avoid the repercussions of past mistakes.

The only way that I could control my lust was to masturbate. I couldn't have the person I wanted so I would fantasize about the things I would like to do with them; it did not matter whether they were male or female.

I would be so thirsty for sex that I had to quench this desire in some way. I had to have sex.

At times my mind was going crazy and I would call my boyfriend and ask when I was going to see him. I was going through hell in my body. I released myself through pornography which led to more lusting and masturbation, but it was better than sleeping with a man or woman.

Some people find it hard to fight their spirits, and urges and give in to sleeping around.

I don't belittle them; some of us are simply more resilient, and I had the strength of God supporting me. Although I had backslidden after giving my life to Him at a young age, I consistently sought His help, acknowledging that I wasn't my true self.

Additionally, my mother and other older women would pray for me.

In my experiences; I have learned that lusting leads to seduction.

When I finally get the attention of that person I've been lusting after, I now turn on my art of seducing them in order to fulfill my desire.

Maybe your sexual desire isn't something he or she would try so you seduce them with your words, actions, gifts, or money. Now the spirit of seduction is working in your life. You won't stop seducing until you get what you want or if you don't get it, you stop and move on to another person.

In movies, the scenario often unfolds with a man pursuing a woman or vice versa, leading to a moment of seduction. This typically involves the woman in seductive lingerie or the man revealing his muscular abs.

However, such scenes can take a dark turn if resistance is met, potentially resulting in rape or murder. The spirit of lust entices individuals into sinful actions and leads them to engage in behaviors they shouldn't.

This is reminiscent of the story of Eve in Genesis 3:6, where she succumbed to the allure of the forbidden tree, seeing it as good for food, pleasant to the eyes, and desirable for wisdom. She ate the fruit and gave it to her husband, leading them into disobedience.

I wanted so bad to get a lap dance from a man and when I went to Atlantic City for one of my birthdays before I got saved. I found out about an exotic men group performing at club and treated myself to the VIP package and I surely had fun.

Lust is a powerful and dangerous sin. God had to delivered me from the spirit of lust and seduction. I can see woman naked or in clothes and have no desire for her. I can see a man in uniform or suit or looks good or naked and I don't want him. I only have the desire for my husband.

At this point; I could compliment a man and leave it at that.

I could tell any man "You look good."

Maybe he will be good in bed, but I was not going to ruin my life by finding out.

I made a promise to God first then my husband that I would not cheat and I'm not breaking that vow.

Chapter Nine

FLESH-LUST

Lessons

❖ The lust of the flesh isn't good and will destroy your life.

❖ Don't give your flesh everything it desires for not all things are good for it.

❖ Lust can cause you to hate yourself when you can't fulfill your desire.

❖ Lust can cause you to lose your hope, mind and life.

❖ Your flesh will fight against the Holy Spirit and you have to resist.

❖ Don't let the lust of your flesh overpower you.

❖ Don't let your flesh cause you to hurt yourself and/or others.

❖ Sanctify your flesh with the Word of God.

❖ Don't let anyone force you to give into their fleshy desires

Chapter Nine

'MY FLESH'

- ❖ Holy Spirit, please help me not give into my lustful desires in the name of Jesus Christ.

- ❖ Holy Spirit help me not to lust after a man or woman.

- ❖ Holy Spirit, I need your help to overcome my weakness of lusting after another person's wife or husband, in the name of Jesus

- ❖ I renounce the relationship I have with you spirit of lust, in the name of Jesus Christ.

- ❖ I bind up you spirit of lust in the name of Jesus Christ.

- ❖ I command you spirit of lust to loose me in the name of Jesus Christ.

- ❖ I send you spirit of lust to the pit of hell and never to return to my life, in the name of Jesus Christ.

- ❖ Lord, I thank You in the name of Jesus Christ for setting me from free from the bondage of the spirit of lust.

Lord, I surrender my desires, my weaknesses, and my sinful inclinations to You. I commit my mind, my thoughts, and my actions to You.

I pray for the power of Your Holy Spirit to dwell within me, enabling me to resist the temptations that seek to lead me astray. Grant me discernment to recognize the schemes of the enemy and the strength to stand firm in Your truth.

I claim the promise of Your Word that says, "No temptation has overtaken you except what is common to mankind. And God is faithful; he will not let you be tempted beyond what you can bear.

But when you are tempted, he will also provide a way out so that you can endure it" (1 Corinthians 10:13, NIV). Strengthen me, Lord, to take hold of the way of escape that You provide.
May Your strength be made perfect in my weakness. In the name of Jesus Christ, I pray. Amen

Reflections

Heavenly Father,

I come before You, acknowledging my weaknesses and the struggles I face with the lusts of the flesh. Your Word reminds me that the spirit is willing, but the flesh is weak. I earnestly seek Your strength and guidance in overcoming these temptations that entangle me.

I thank you for Your forgiveness for the times I have succumbed to the allure of the flesh. Create in me a clean heart, O God, and renew a right spirit within me.

Thank you for filling me with Your love, joy, and peace, and let the fruits of the Spirit flourish within me. Helping me to fix my eyes on Jesus, the author, and perfector of my faith.

Thank You, Lord, for Your grace that is sufficient for me. I trust in Your power to deliver me from the bondage of the lusts of the flesh.

Chapter Ten

FRUSTRATED FROM CHURCH HURT

Attending church posed a challenge for me due to past hurts from both my family and fellow church members.

The struggle intensified because I felt limited in my participation due to my limited connection with the Holy Spirit.

Despite my declaration to serve God, I found myself falling back into behaviors contrary to His commandments. The internal conflict made church seem dull, as I grappled with the enjoyment of sin while still desiring to please God

God doesn't play when it comes to attending church.

When God called me to serve, I faced the dilemma of choosing a church. I explored a Pentecostal congregation near my home and another affiliated with a family member. However, the wounds from my family made it difficult to consider their church.

Interestingly, God orchestrated circumstances that led my family member to establish a church conveniently close to my apartment. It became evident that God was serious about my involvement in a church community.

During my college days, I attended classes during the day and made an effort to go to church in the evenings.

I specially made sure I attended the night services. There was a special service that spanned a few days, and I felt compelled to invite my sister Sashikia. However, I hesitated, fearing her refusal.

To my surprise, on the last night, she informed me that she would join me in attending church. From that point on, we embarked on a journey of serving God together, and months later, my older sister Shelly-Ann also dedicated her life to God.

On a memorable night during a church service featuring a visiting Bishop, I found myself dancing in worship.

A family member approached me, sharing that the Bishop had observed something significant about my feet and mentioned that I was his family.

Subsequently, I was informed that the Bishop was requesting a picture, name, birthday, and another detail, along with a fee of $300. Another family member confirmed the authenticity of the request.

I was struggling and could not get out of this by myself.

I know I was struggling for years, internally longing to break free from my challenges. When presented with an opportunity to seek guidance, I was both surprised and skeptical.

The process seemed reminiscent of practices like witchcraft or obeah, commonly associated with seeking insights from a reader man in Jamaica.

Despite my reservations, I provided the requested money of $300 and wrote down the required information. I insisted on meeting the Bishop in person before proceeding further.

In the course of our meeting, the Bishop revealed details that were undeniably accurate, thereby lending credibility to his purported abilities. Nonetheless, some of his predictions about potential future actions on my part left me perplexed.

In an effort to gain better understanding and clarity, I requested permission to record our conversation, aiming to review the information he provided at a later time.

One thing that got me was a man set a sex demon on me. I asked if he could tell me who it was, but he didn't to avoid problems. There was a smell of incense being burned in the church, and it didn't smell good.

As a young Christian seeking guidance, I found myself questioning why the Bishop was employing a specific method instead of simply offering prayers. Despite my uncertainty, I was scheduled for another meeting with him.

Meanwhile, my church, with close ties to the Pastor, attended a few of the Bishop's services.

Unexpectedly, the Pastor introduced me to an Elder residing in the Caribbean Island of Antigua. On a Friday, the Pastor informed me that the Elder would speak to me the following Saturday, emphasizing that he couldn't assist me with the challenges I was facing.

The news left me surprised, wondering why the Pastor directed me to someone else.

I speculated that perhaps the Pastor felt unequipped to address my family issues and sought assistance from someone more qualified in handling such problems.

Deception upon Deception

On that Saturday night, an unfortunate incident occurred, resulting in the shooting and death of the Bishop. In the aftermath, I learned that there were allegations of wrongdoing associated with him, potentially contributing to the tragic outcome.

Reflecting on the situation, I saw it as God's protection, preventing me from becoming deeply involved with the Bishop and potentially exposing myself to more harmful influences than I was already dealing with.

While the Bishop displayed a friendly and jovial demeanor, some of the principles and practices he embraced were really inappropriate.

An example of this was when he advised someone close to me to wash off in the sea—a practice commonly associated with obeah in Jamaica, a belief system that involves seeking purification through sea water.

In contrast, I believe in the power of Jesus Christ to lift curses through prayer rather than relying on sea water for spiritual cleansing.

The incident served as a stark reminder of the importance of discernment and adherence to biblical principles.

The Elder disclosed that he was in the midst of divorce proceedings, assuring me that he was not currently married. He requested financial assistance for the divorce process, and I, trusting in our supposed relationship, gave him what he asked for.

Our relationship was to be kept secret, and as a result, I turned to prayer, seeking God's guidance in this complex situation.

Over time, I found myself sending him monthly contributions, including items in barrels and financial support. The Elder deceived me, saying that sowing this money would bring healing and deliverance to myself and my family.

I was naïve and entrusted him with my retirement savings, believing that he was channeling the funds to the main church headquarters in Nigeria as he said he would.

Looking back, I now see how deceptive he was and I now realize the importance of discernment and seeking wise counsel in matters of the heart and finances.

At times, he displayed greatness, which initially made it difficult to recognize his deception.

He encouraged me to meditate on the scriptures and advised me not to let anyone hinder me from following God's Word.

At a certain point, I planned to meet the Elder in person by traveling to his country, but the meeting fell through due to unforeseen circumstances he claimed had occurred. Despite my concerns, I didn't press further.

It was during this time that a Christian doctor warned me about the Elder, stating that he had a history of using young ladies. When I shared this with him, he responded by instructing me not to see that doctor again.

I needed guidance

Seeking divine guidance, an Evangelist friend conveyed a message from God, stating that the man I was dating was using me and not meant for me. God had someone else in mind for my future.

This revelation left me upset, prompting me to confront the Elder about what God had revealed to him regarding our relationship. He admitted that God had told him I wouldn't be his wife, but he confessed to wanting to continue trying against God's guidance.

As we discontinued in our relationship, the Elder started showing controlling behavior. He demanded detailed accounts of my activities, conversations, and even insisted that I shouldn't make decisions without consulting him.

It became apparent that he sought to control not only my actions but also my finances.

His constant assertions of seeing into my life created a sense of fear, making me question if he was always monitoring my every move, thereby diverting my focus from God to his influence.

The pain of my experiences led me to seek solace in writing letters to God, pouring out my heart and asking for His guidance.

A prophetess visiting the church conveyed a message that resonated with me — that I needed to let go of the hurt caused by the Elder and resume writing letters to God.

However, this prophetess also shared messages that seemed inconsistent and even conflicting. She suggested that God wanted me to remain in the army and become a nurse, a direction that didn't align with my preferences and past experiences.

Moreover, there were instances where she revealed personal secrets I had confided in her, breaching the trust I had placed in her.

Amidst the drama and confusion in the church, the Pastor informed me that the Elder was meant to bring me to a certain point, and then the Pastor would take over.

This revelation left me confused, especially considering the Elder's influence over the Pastor, even guiding him on sermon topics.

A dream further added to my confusion, depicting a scene where the church faced judgment from the Pastor and another man, with an angel watching.

Subsequently, a church meeting took place, leading to the expulsion of those who opposed the Pastor's actions.

This departure left me questioning whether this was truly God's church, as Jesus, in the Bible, confronted wrongdoing within the temple but never expelled His children for disagreements.

The scriptural reference from John 2:13-16 served as a reminder that Jesus confronted wrongdoing in the temple but didn't cast out those who belonged to Him.

"And the Jews' Passover was at hand, and Jesus went up to Jerusalem. And found in the temple those that sold oxen and sheep and doves, and the changers of money sitting: And when he had made a scourge of small cords, he drove them all out of the temple, and the sheep, and the oxen; and poured out the changers' money, and overthrew the tables; And said unto them that sold doves, Take these things hence; make not my Father's house an house of merchandise."

This prompted me to reflect on the authenticity of the church's actions and the need for a place of worship guided by love and understanding rather than exclusion.

Starting all over in a new church

Now, that some of us had been kicked out of the church; we decided to begin a new church.

Among our company was a minister who felt the call to become a Pastor. Interestingly, this same Elder was chosen to be the overseer for our newly formed congregation.

Unfortunately, I observed individuals being ordained simply because this Elder sought inappropriate relationships with them or planned to. The disappointment and pain from my previous church, coupled with these disheartening experiences in the new one, led me to express my frustration to God.

I declared that I wouldn't convey any more messages to people; I no longer wished to prophesy. Before all the heartache began, I had been actively evangelizing.

It seemed like my role had been reduced to recording the services and distributing the records or sharing them on social media. I questioned what more I could contribute.

Eventually, I was encouraged to join the praise team. Throughout this period, I grappled with emotional pain but remained steadfast in my commitment to serve God.

There was a concerning situation involving a girl in the church who started talking to the Elder. The church organized a care package for the Elder, and she got him some requested items.

I recalled a similar experience when he had done the same thing to me, and her behavior strongly suggested that something was happening between them.

She had borrowed something from someone close to me, and I sensed that something was amiss, especially after she visited the Elder.

One day, I gathered the courage to ask him if he was dating her, and he confirmed it. He shared that the Lord had guided him to be with her.

Upon hearing this, I couldn't help but reflect on the rumors from the former church meeting where someone mentioned that they were dating.

I expressed my concern, noting that the Lord couldn't lead someone to be with another young woman in the church when they were already married.

The girl's behavior towards me changed, and she began to compete with me during praise and worship services. Eventually, she left the church, severed ties with her best friend, me, and others because of the Elder. I pray that she is currently serving God.

I loved to worship the Lord

Continuing to attend church and engage in the work of God, I found myself struggling with the challenge of worshiping alongside individuals who had been against me.

Our journey led us to the Caribbean Island of Antigua, where the Elder resides, for a convention. During this event, I observed a young girl paying a visit to him.

Oh, this man was after the young girls in church and he had the nerve to ask me if I would have had sex with him if he wanted.

I immediately; without reservation, looked him straight in his eye and said; "no!"

On a day when I was sick and weak during the visit, he didn't come to me and offer a prayer, even though I was right there at his home. Instead, he briefly inquired about my well-being and proceeded to speak negatively about the Pastor from the church we had visited for the convention to two other leaders.

Later on, he took members from that Pastor's church to start a new church. This Elder spread falsehoods about me to both members and leaders, leading to a strained or severed relationship between us.

Exercising Caution

As leaders, it is crucial to exercise caution when appointing individuals to oversee or lead specific aspects of a ministry. Some may carry a Jezebel spirit, seeking to poison the minds of church members and draw them away. Both leaders and members must be diligent in prayer, consistently seeking God's protection for the ministry.

The Jezebel spirit is known to introduce elements of divination and sexual perversion into the fabric of a ministry. To safeguard the integrity of the church, it is essential to stay vigilant, relying on prayer as a powerful tool to discern and resist such influences.

Through continual communion with God, leaders and members can fortify the spiritual boundaries of the ministry, ensuring it remains a place of purity, devotion, and genuine worship.

While receiving therapy for military injuries back home in the States, I engaged in fervent prayer and worship. Unbeknownst to me, I spoke in tongues extensively, not fully comprehending that I possessed the gift.

These moments of tongue-speaking could last for extended periods, sometimes up to an hour, with each instance being different.

I felt a positive connection during these sessions, often experiencing a sense of release, even to the point of physically falling to the side of my altar while praying on my knees.

However, during a convention service, the Elder overheard me speaking in tongues and whispered to me, instructing me to cease. He asserted that my tongues were demonic.

He instilled fear of speaking in tongues in me.

Reluctant to share this experience, especially given the authoritative figure's declaration, I refrained from speaking in tongues thereafter. Even when prompted by the Holy Spirit, I suppressed the urge, choosing not to express this spiritual gift.

I was resisting the promptings of the Holy Spirit. Each time He gave me words to speak, I remained silent, and if even a sound escaped during prayer, I halted my prayer.

This behavior could be likened to quenching the Holy Spirit, as mentioned in 1 Thessalonians 5:19:

"Do not quench the Spirit."

I asked permission from the Elder to speak, but he denied it. Soon after, I began having disturbing dreams where both he and the Pastor appeared in sinister forms, attempting to harm me.

These dreams persisted for months, driven by my reluctance to speak in tongues, as the Elder had forbidden it, leading to demonic attacks.

In my ignorance, I hesitated to share my struggles with the Pastor as the Elder instructed secrecy. Feeling trapped, I cried out to God for deliverance, questioning why I couldn't be set free while adhering to the Elder's restrictions.

During a special service led by Prophetess Fire, she ministered to me, urging me to speak in tongues. As I obeyed, I experienced liberation, and Prophetess Fire revealed the nature of the tongues to the members.

Confiding in the Pastor, I disclosed the Elder's actions, including his desire to marry me and the financial transactions.

This revelation exposed multiple instances of inappropriate behavior towards other females, prompting the need to escalate the issue to the main overseer in Nigeria.

Under the Elder's influence, I wore a bracelet he insisted on, claiming it provided protection. When it broke, I transformed it into a pendant, still bound by his control.

God intervened, breaking the bracelet to free me from his manipulative powers, though I initially failed to recognize it.

Finally Breaking Free

Over time, I distanced myself from the Elder, breaking the cycle of mind control. As I ceased sharing personal details with him, my life began to improve.

I refrained from informing him about job interviews and relationships, witnessing positive outcomes. I even discarded the broken bracelet as a symbolic act of breaking free from his influence.

Keep your friends close and your enemies closer

Even those who used to inquire about my marriage plans distanced themselves when I got engaged. A girl I considered a friend, whom I had taken to church, shopped with, and confided in during my dating period, betrayed me.

The hurt deepened as church members, who pretended to be supportive and caring, made jokes about me not getting married. Years before my engagement, during a service, I openly expressed my desire for God to provide me with a husband, only to be met with laughter.

My cousins, whom I had hosted in my home, shared my bed, and cooked for, revealed a different side of themselves, severing ties after learning of my engagement.

In the midst of this pain, a male Apostle encouraged me to remain faithful, acknowledging the challenges I faced in the church.

Members of the praise team gradually left, leaving only two of us. Unbeknownst to me, the remaining member, a female, was orchestrating my removal.

Despite leading a worship session effectively and earning recognition from a visiting Pastor, the Associate Pastor called a meeting, even for those uninterested in the team.

The Associate Pastor in charge of the praise and worship team, was also my cousin, who harbored resentment towards me and sought to remove me from the team.

During the meeting, I was forbidden from drinking water during praise and worship. I resisted, questioning the logic of denying water for a dry throat or discomfort.

The situation escalated, and I realized that everyone, even those who previously drank water during worship breaks, was against me.

Through dreams and visions, God revealed that my cousin, the Associate Pastor, played a role in splitting the church.

Keeping these insights to myself, I declined hugs from those who had betrayed me after the service, recalling the warnings given by the Lord in my visions.

There's a Problem with the Order in the Church

The two pastors at the church were experiencing difficulties, with the Elder dictating instructions to the Associate Pastor.

It seemed perplexing that members preferred to live in sin and go against God's teachings.

Eventually, the Senior Pastor decided to leave, and those adhering to righteous living, including myself, also departed. This move allowed me to break free from the spiritual attacks from both the former church and the Elder.

However, I neglected to pray off the lingering spiritual influences, leading to challenges. Leaving a church often exposes individuals to spiritual attacks from unclean spirits associated with people from that church.

The new church initially seemed promising until I advised the pastor, who was a friend, not to speak negatively about someone else. Despite my intention to be honest and supportive, I was labeled disloyal.

Following this incident, various aspects of my involvement came under criticism, but I continued attending church with the conviction that my service was dedicated to God, not to man.

Circumstances changed, and I couldn't attend church every Sunday as I had done in the past due to limitations in rental space for services and the impact of Covid-19.

Nothing or No One can take me from the Presence of God

Before that nothing could stop me from going to church on a Sunday or Bible Study rain or snow I was going to church. When my vehicle broke down, I couldn't go to praise and worship practice, but Sunday service I was in church.

I was kind to people so God provided the financial means through my mother's friend and a close army friend to facilitate the repair of my vehicle.

I felt God's protective hand because of my unwavering commitment to faithfully serve Him.

Despite facing challenges, such as attending an all-night prayer meeting during a snowstorm and navigating back from Long Island to the Bronx at 5:00 am, I trusted in God's guidance. Few of us were in my blessed Jeep, and God ensured a safe journey home.

On another occasion, heavy rain threatened to cause me to lose control of the Jeep. Yet, I felt a divine force take over the steering wheel, guiding the vehicle out of the water as we approached the Throngs Neck Bridge. Once we were safe, the force released the steering wheel.

Grateful for God's intervention, I silently thanked Him, later sharing the testimony in church the following Sunday. While I couldn't disclose to the Jeep's occupants that it wasn't me driving through the water, I wanted to acknowledge and express my gratitude for the divine assistance.

It's Hard Serving God when you are Hurting

It is hard serving God when some of the leaders are the one hurting you and pushing you out of church. Being in church and getting hurt from family members who claim they are representing is like someone putting a knife to your throat and you are holding their hand and trying to stop them.

I cried many nights begging God to help me. Why is not the church a place of help and not hurt? I felt like I was being judged because of my past life issues before I became a Christian.

I didn't even want to be hugged by the females and it took me a while to do that. I felt used and not loved. Like persons only spoke to me for a money or what I could do for them.

I put up a person from Antigua and that person betrayed me. I made sacrifices for the ministries and I got a slap in my face. You see regardless of those things and how hurt I was, I never regretted being kind and loving. All I did was for God. I loved God and was happy to help Him through the use of my gifts.

I refused to let those who had hurt me do so again. Choosing to forgive them, I moved on and embraced my life. Following God's guidance to forgive, I remembered Mark 11:26,

> *"But if ye do not forgive, neither will your Father which is in heaven forgive your trespasses."*

There were times when I wanted to kill myself even though I was going church. The hurt was so much. The devil used this opportunity to whisper voices to me that no one loves me and to look how they treat me.

I wasn't perfect but I was angry at some people. I yelled at them if they said anything to me. God had to take that temper from me.

Talk about a lion roaring. I went into depression and hated seeing church members or talking to them. I didn't want to be around them. If I complained to a leader about some of the things, I would get the blame so I shut my mouth and stopped speaking about it.

I cried at the altar, always seeking prayer for I needed help. No one knows how deep inside I wanted my life to just end and go home to be with God.

One night I was so tired of fighting men in my dream after three men came to kill me, I just said go ahead and kill me, I'm going home to be with my father (that is God).

I heard a voice said no, not yet there is work for me to do.

Friends, I was ready to go to heaven for I was tired of fighting physically and spiritually.

One evening, as I headed to church with my Bluetooth headset on, I suddenly felt a burning sensation and an inexplicable urge to cough. Despite the headset having an open front, making it seemingly impossible to cause discomfort, it began to feel like it was attacking me.

I was accompanied by my mother, and upon sharing my experience with her, I quickly removed the headset. From that day on, I refrained from wearing it around my neck out of fear, as it had left a noticeable mark.

Subsequently, I encountered similar sensations a few more times, especially when approaching the church building, leaving my body feeling peculiar.

I used to believe that a man, being a Christian, would be different from a sinful man. However, I soon realized that if a Christian man is not saved and delivered from demonic spirits, he is essentially just like a sinner.

The only difference is that he is dressed in a church suit and attending church services (a wolf in sheep's clothing).

One man, aware of my financial standing, claimed that God revealed he was meant to be my husband. I wasn't desperate enough to accept such a proposition. Another man attempted to pursue me while already dating another church sister – a behavior I found questionable.

As believers, we are called to be as harmless as doves and as cunning as serpents, as stated in Matthew 10:16:

"Behold, I send you forth as sheep in the midst of wolves: be ye therefore wise as serpents, and harmless as doves."

God revealed to me the hidden motives of men playing games, prompting me to pray for clarity about their true intentions.

Recognizing that everyone has weaknesses requiring God's assistance, I've come to understand that the church has some individuals seeking help or those whom God has delivered from various demons, much like Mary Magdalene in Luke 8:2:

"And certain women, which had been healed of evil spirits and infirmities, Mary called Magdalene, out of whom went seven devils."

The church, I've realized, is a battleground where demonic spirits wage war against Angels and the Holy Spirit. It's crucial to navigate carefully, as there are hidden dangers waiting to attack, akin to snipers or landmines.

Despite the challenges, attending church for healing or deliverance can be transformative.

Unlike a hospital where one might return home still unwell,

church offers the possibility of leaving healed and delivered from tormenting demons.

Personally, I experienced freedom from evil spirits during a church service through worship, prayer, or the laying on of hands. It's a reminder that you receive what you seek in church, and regardless of the hurts caused by people, one must remain faithful to God.

The journey won't be easy, as evidenced by the mistreatment of Jesus Christ, who was eventually killed. May no one succumb to self-destruction due to church hurts, in the name of Jesus.

Chapter Ten

FRUSTRATED FROM CHURCH HURT

Lessons

- Be led the Holy Spirit not by man.

- Be obedient to the voice of God.

- Live by the commandments of God not by man's ways or your fleshy ways.

- Reject men and the devil deceptive ways and pursue God's ways.

- Allow the Holy Spirit to teach you and seek him daily for directions.

- Don't sleep with man or woman to get a position in church. What is in the dark will come to the light.

- Work out your own salvation with fear and trembling and God's help.

- Don't be desperate to be seen by people in church.

- Live an honest and trustworthy life.

- Preserve your body for your husband or wife.

- Study the word of God, daily.

- Don't join any cults or be a partaker of witchcraft in church or otherwise.

- Try the spirit of man by the Spirit of God.

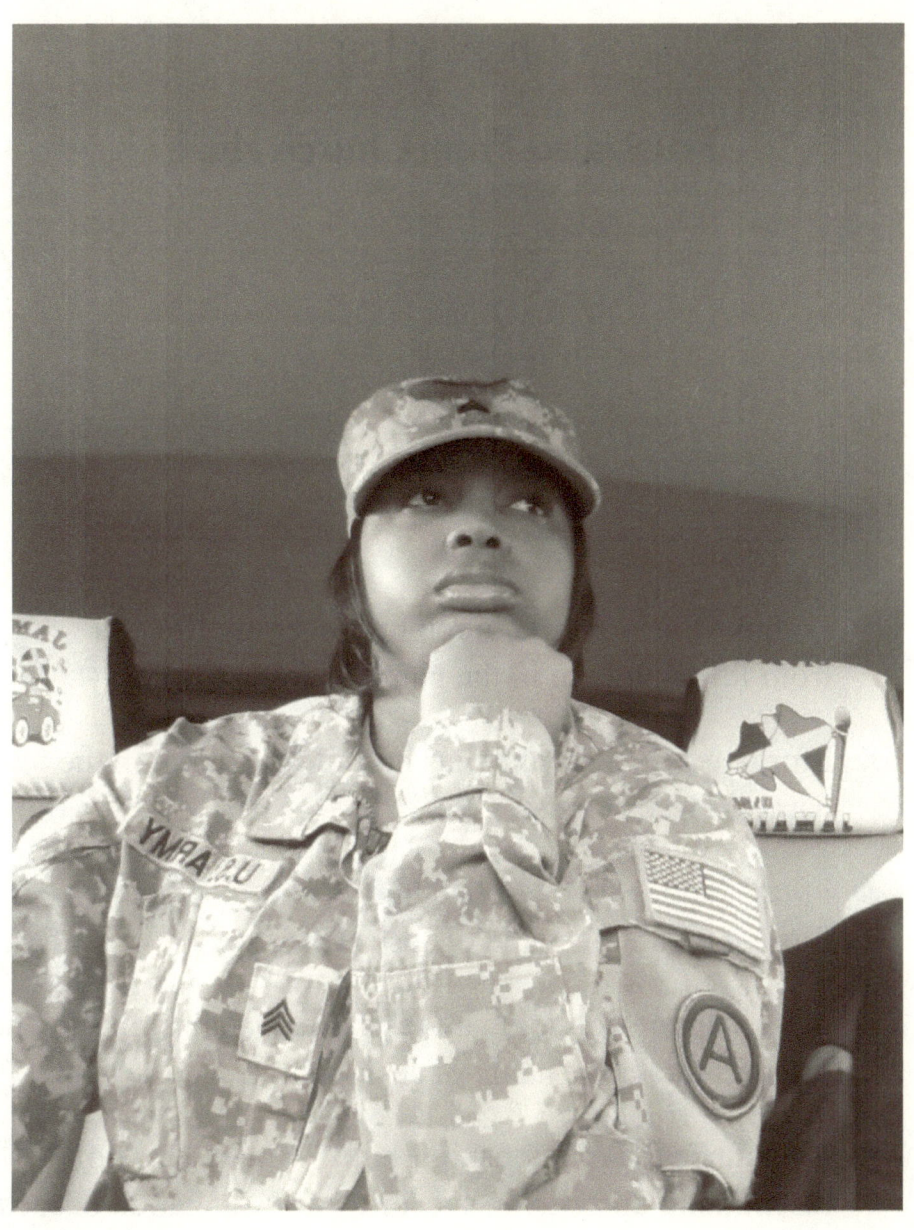

Chapter Ten

Frustrated From Church Hurt

❖ I rebuke the spirit of church hurt over my life and from following me in the name of Jesus Christ.

❖ I forgive every one that has hurt me in church in the name of Jesus Christ.

❖ I pray the people that I had hurt in church would forgive me in the name of Jesus Christ.

❖ Lord help me not hold any resentment against those who has hurt me in the name of Jesus Christ.

❖ I renounce the relationship I built with the spirit of resentment, unforgiveness, hurt, pain and hatred because of church hurt in the name of Jesus Christ.

❖ I lose myself from the spirit of resentment, unforgiveness, church hurt, pain and hatred in the name of Jesus Christ.

❖ I command the spirit of resentment, unforgiveness, church hurt, pain and hatred to get out of body and life and go to the pit of hell, in the name of Jesus Christ and never return to my life.

❖ I reject and cast the spirt of betrayal and deception out of life, in the name of Jesus Christ.

❖ The spirit of fear will not take over my mind in the name of Jesus Christ pertaining to going church.

❖ I pray that the spirit of a sound mind, power and love will operate in my life, in the name of Jesus Christ

Dear Heavenly Father, I come before you with a heavy heart, burdened by the frustration and pain caused by church hurt. Lord, you know the depths of my wounds and the disappointment that has settled in my spirit.

I lift up to you all the hurts, betrayals, and misunderstandings that have taken place within the body of believers.
Father, I ask for your divine comfort and healing to envelop my heart. Grant me the strength to forgive those who have caused me pain, just as you have forgiven me.

Help me release the bitterness and resentment that may have taken root in my soul. Fill me with your peace that surpasses understanding, and let it guard my heart against further distress.

Lord, I pray for a spirit of reconciliation within the church. May

your love and grace permeate the hearts of those who have hurt me, leading to understanding and unity. Help us, as a community of believers, to exemplify your teachings of love, compassion, and forgiveness.

I surrender my hurt and frustration to you, Lord, and ask for a renewed sense of purpose within the church. Guide me in contributing to a healthier, more compassionate community where your love prevails. May your Holy Spirit empower me to navigate the complexities of relationships with grace and humility. In Jesus' name, I pray. Amen.

Reflections

Dear Heavenly Father, thank you for the moments of frustration, you, remind me of your unwavering love and acceptance. Let me find solace in your presence and reassurance in the knowledge that you understand the pain I carry. Strengthen my faith, that I may continue to trust in your perfect plan despite the challenges presented by the actions of others.

Thank you, Lord, for being my refuge and source of healing and bringing beauty from the ashes of my church hurt and use this experience to deepen my reliance on you.

PRAYER, Worship AND FASTING

"When you fast, do not look somber as the hypocrites do, for they disfigure their faces to show others they are fasting. Truly I tell you, they have their reward. But when you fast, put oil on your head and wash your face, so that it will not be obvious to others that you are fasting, but only to your Father, who is unseen; and your Father, who sees what is done in secret, will reward you." (Matthew 6:16-18 NIV):

This scripture emphasizes the importance of sincerity in fasting, doing it as a personal, private devotion to God rather than seeking recognition from others. It encourages maintaining an inward focus on spiritual growth and communion with God during the period of fasting.

I faced considerable difficulty sleeping due to my struggles with insomnia and PTSD from my military service. Throughout the night, I would wake up multiple times, unable to find rest.

My mind raced with numerous thoughts, making it challenging to achieve the sleep I desperately desired. Even attempts to watch a movie on TV proved ineffective in bringing relief.

One night, I made a decision to turn to prayer or read the Bible every time I woke up. This marked the beginning of a transformation in my spiritual life. Despite the dark moments of wrestling with PTSD, I began building a deep and personal relationship with God.

While I had been accustomed to praying in the solitude of my home, I harbored fears of judgment from others if they were to hear me pray in church or elsewhere. Overcoming insecurities and fears took time, but gradually, I learned to let go and express my prayers.

I prayed about various aspects of my life, and this practice became so ingrained that I found myself praying even in my sleep, during meals, while driving, or in the company of others. Whether aloud or in the quiet recesses of my heart, prayer became a constant companion, helping me navigate through the challenges and uncertainties of life.

Pray Without Ceasing

The scripture in 1 Thessalonians 5:17 instructs us to:

"Pray without ceasing."

I took this command to heart and begin maintaining a constant dialogue with God.

Often, I found myself prompted by the Holy Spirit to pray in the midst of conversations. At times, a sense of apprehension would lead me to discreetly pray, even if it meant excusing myself to the bathroom.

I wanted to avoid appearing self-righteous or holier-than-thou, and I was mindful not to quench the Spirit's work.

There were moments when I prayed in tongues, I understand what it meant and other times I didn't comprehend the specific intercessions made by the Holy Spirit. As Romans 8:26 (KJV) states:

"Likewise, the Spirit also helpeth our infirmities: for we know not what we should pray for as we ought: but the Spirit itself maketh intercession for us with groanings which cannot be uttered."

I understood that the Holy Spirit was interceding through me for someone, and if I chose not to pray, He would guide someone else to take my place.

Over time, I released my concerns about how others perceived my prayers or how eloquently they spoke to God. I embraced the idea that prayer is a personal communication with God, and I didn't need to employ fancy or borrowed words.

True prayer, I realized, originates from the heart and isn't a mere repetition of empty words. God desires genuine connection through the Holy Spirit, and authenticity in prayer is paramount. I refused to pretend or fake my prayers, understanding that authenticity is crucial. I let the Holy Spirit lead me in prayer.

In one instance, my teacher in ministry school insisted that I pray, but I resisted. Despite my reluctance, she persisted, suggesting that God might have a purpose for my prayer. Reflecting on her words, I later found myself actively praying for people, realizing that God had indeed called me to this role.I Found Peace Through Praying to my Heavenly Father

I used to experience intense fear and paranoia, and my peace came from prayer. Praying was not just a routine for me; it was a lifeline because I desperately needed help. My prayer focus was on seeking freedom from the influence of evil spirits.

Psalm 23, "The Lord is my shepherd," became my go-to scripture. Reciting these verses brought a sense of safety and tranquility, serving as a source of comfort during challenging times.

The Lord is my shepherd; I shall not want.

He maketh me to lie down in green pastures: he leadeth me beside the still waters.

He restoreth my soul: he leadeth me in the paths of righteousness for his name's sake.

Yea, though I walk through the valley of the shadow of death, I will fear no evil: for thou art with me; thy rod and thy staff they comfort me.

Thou preparest a table before me in the presence of mine enemies: thou anointest my head with oil; my cup runneth over.

Surely goodness and mercy shall follow me all the days of my life: and I will dwell in the house of the Lord forever.

Prayer, for me, was more than a spiritual practice; it was my sustenance and the means through which I connected with God.

It was my way of reaching out to Him, confident that He would hear and respond.

My belief in the effectiveness of prayer was unwavering, and I cherished the moments when I poured out my heart to God. Even in my childhood, I engaged in heartfelt conversations with Him, expressing my emotions about feeling hated and hurt by others.

During moments of solitude, I would silently communicate with God, earnestly seeking His help to overcome my inner struggles. My prayers were filled with requests for guidance— to prevent myself from becoming rude or engaging in negative behaviors, to address the speech difficulties I struggled with, and to alleviate the anxiety that weighed heavily on me.

In Those Intimate Conversations With God, I Found A Refuge And A Path Toward Inner Peace.

Now I Take My Pains and Grievances to God

No one knows me better than my Heavenly Father. Prayer serves as the bridge that draws me closer to God, allowing me to enter His presence. Through prayer, I experience the anointing of God, and without it, I find myself lacking in both substance and joy. Communicating with my Father, Jehovah, through prayer brings me a profound sense of joy.

When people inflict pain upon me, my recourse is to take my grievances to God in prayer.

I entrust those who hurt me into His care, for His word in Romans 12:19 KJV declares that vengeance belongs to Him:

"Dearly beloved, avenge not yourselves, but rather give place unto wrath: for it is written, Vengeance is mine; I will repay, saith the Lord"

I relinquish the need to engage in physical battles, knowing that God, my defender, fights on my behalf spiritually. He possesses complete knowledge of my enemies, discerning the perfect time to intervene and grant me victory.

In prayer, I yield control of my life to God, providing Him with the opportunity to take charge.

As His creation, we were given dominion over the earth, as stated in Genesis 1:26 (ESV):

"Then God said, 'Let us make man in our image, after our likeness. And let them have dominion over the fish of the sea and over the birds of the heavens and over the livestock and over all the earth and over every creeping thing that creeps on the earth.'"

This is the unchanging word of God.

I Now Take My Battles to the Lord

Early in my relationship with my husband, I conveyed a sincere message: 'if he were to hurt me, I would take the matter to my Heavenly Father, Jehovah, through prayer.'

While it may have sounded like a warning, I was serious about seeking God's divine intervention on the behalf of my relationship with my husband.

This principle applies universally, I'm not going to be prejudice regardless of their title or religious affiliation. It doesn't matter whether they are an Apostle, Bishop, Christian, or unsaved. I make no distinctions; I am bringing everyone to my Father for

His intervention.

Although I do seek prayer support from others, I am selective about whom I approach. Some individuals, regrettably, harbor ill intentions and may betray my trust by spreading personal matters. Thus, I exercise discernment in choosing those to whom I entrust my prayer requests.

Knowing whom to ask for prayer and when to seek it is a crucial aspect of navigating our spiritual journey.

There are instances when the magnitude of the battle necessitates enlisting the support of others in prayer. Recognizing the power of collective prayer, I have reached out to family, friends, and even social media acquaintances as guided by the Holy Spirit.

I have also experienced moments where I dreamt about people and felt compelled to intercede on their behalf—a calling from God to pray for others.

My commitment to prayer extends beyond Christians to include the unsaved, musicians, actors, government leaders, cities, countries and even those who may be considered enemies. Matthew 5:44 (KJV) guides me:

"But I say unto you, Love your enemies, bless them that curse you, do good to them that hate you, and pray for them which despitefully use you, and persecute you."

While we may desire God's vengeance, we are instructed to pray for transformation in the lives of those who oppose us. As Christians, we face persecution from those who reject God, yet we are called to intercede for them.

I Surrender All To God's Control

Discovering the power of prayer during my period of illness and subsequent healing led me to a profound revelation: I possessed spiritual gifts, including the gifts of healing, diverse tongues, prophecy, and others. As 1 Corinthians 12:10 (KJV) states:

"to another the working of miracles; to another prophecy; to another discerning of spirits; to another divers kinds of tongues; to another the interpretation of tongues."

It was through prayer that these gifts were unveiled to me, a result of my connection to Jehovah, my Creator, and the revelation by His Holy Spirit of the divine endowments within me.

Witnessing the manifestation of my spiritual gifts during moments of prayer and consistent seeking of God's presence left me in awe. It became clear to me that prayer serves as the gateway through which God enters our lives and works through us.

The spiritual door to God opens during prayer, providing an avenue for Him to reveal Himself and His gifts to those who seek Him diligently. The realization that prayer is the key to unlocking spiritual gifts would inspire more people to devote time to prayer and communion with God.

From prayer, our spiritual gifts are birthed, and the anointing is sustained. Understanding this truth has become a source of strength for me and will continue to be so. It is within the realm of prayer that I have encountered the richness of my spiritual gifts, and it remains an ongoing journey of connection and revelation with my Creator.

Praying in Unknown Tongues

There is often confusion when I engage in praying in my unknown tongues.

It's important to distinguish between the personal unknown tongues through which I communicate with God and the diverse unknown tongues (languages) He uses me to pray for various issues and against different demonic forces.

When I speak in my personal unknown tongues, it is a private communication with God, as highlighted in 1 Corinthians 14:2 (KJV):

"For he that speaketh in an unknown tongue speaketh not unto men, but unto God: for no man understandeth him; howbeit in the spirit he speaketh mysteries."

In some instances, I may be praying for someone, and they understand the language I'm speaking, even if it is not a language I personally know. God allows me to pray in the specific tongues that the person can comprehend, making the communication effective.

After a prayer session, someone approached me and mentioned that I had spoken in their native language, sharing with me the content of what I had said.

My ability to speak in various tongues extends beyond language barriers. This includes commanding Angels or addressing demonic forces in their respective languages, as these spiritual entities comprehend the language of the unknown tongues.

It's crucial to emphasize that my use of unknown tongues is not intended to evoke fear. Instead, it is a divine gift that allows me to communicate with God on a profound level.

At times, the Lord grants me the interpretation of what I am saying or singing in tongues, as mentioned in 1 Corinthians 14:15 (KJV):

"What is it then? I will pray with the spirit, and I will pray with the understanding also: I will sing with the spirit, and I will sing with the understanding also."

This dual communication—spiritual and with understanding—enhances the depth and effectiveness of my prayers.

Prayer is the Greatest Weapon We Have to Fight Against the Enemy

I set aside regular times for prayer. I follow the example of the Hebrew boys in the Bible; Daniel, Shadrach, Meshach, and Abednego—both in the morning, afternoon, evening, and at various other times.

Over time, prayer has become an important part of my daily routine, forming the foundation of a vibrant prayer life.

Through prayer, a portal opens to the spiritual realm, where the Lord reveals insights about demons, malevolent forces, angels, individuals to intercede for, and glimpses of past and future events.

Prayer is an extraordinary weapon in our arsenal against the enemy. Unlike carrying a cumbersome bag with weapons, prayer is accessible at any time.

There's no need to fumble for instructions on how to draw, pull a trigger, or worry about its effectiveness. In the face of the enemy's onslaught or the onset of illness, a simple act of opening one's mouth in prayer yields answers.

As mentioned earlier, prayer grants me the ability to perceive the spiritual realm, offering glimpses of both angels and demons. Delving deeper into prayer intensifies these spiritual insights.

While some revelations may evoke fear, others bring profound joy. I recall an instance where I encountered a frightening demon during prayer, prompting me to open my eyes.

In response, I told the Lord that, next time, I would approach such experiences with greater composure, acknowledging the depth of revelation that prayer can bring.

While deployed in Kuwait and Baghdad, prayer became my steadfast ally. I continuously sought God's protection against the adversaries of my country. With unwavering faith in my Heavenly Father, He safely guided me back home.

Before I got married, I would pray in the night without any distraction, solely focusing on God.

I recall hearing a demonic voice criticizing my devotion, saying I prayed excessively. My husband would inquire about my whereabouts if I left the bed to pray, and even if I felt tired, I would still rise to pray because it was my source of strength.

I arranged prayer altars in various locations around the house, ensuring that I could commune with God anywhere, as He was welcomed in every corner of our home.

WORSHIP

Worshipping is another great way to get closer to God. I love to sing and glorify God. It became a comfort to my soul other prayer that if I found myself sad, I would sing a song to uplift myself. When I don't remember the words of the songs, I add my own words and as times goes by the Holy Spirit gave me words for my own song.

I would also wake up with my spirit man singing a song and continue singing it. I have set a side time in my schedule to worship God so I can be in his presence.

I loveeee to dance and when I do I feel like I am dancing for God and no one else matter. I don't care what I look like with my dance I just dance for God and let the Holy Spirit take over.

Having the Holy Spirit take over my worship and dancing is powerful just as prayer. Dancing in the spirit brings healing and deliverance. My dance is not a regular dance, and most people know me by my dancing on social media.

Some Christians understand when I'm dancing in my spirit and there is a change in atmosphere. There were times when I danced at my former church my sister Sashikia watched me to ensure I didn't hit into the furniture because when the Holy Spirit takes over. I close my eyes and just let Him move me.

I had learned over the years to control my flesh when the power of the Holy Spirit is working in me.

FASTING

"Even now," declares the Lord, "return to me with all your heart, with fasting and weeping and mourning." (Joel 2:12 NIV)

Fasting is a voluntary abstention from food, drink, or other physical needs for a set period of time. It is often done for religious, spiritual, or health reasons. Fasting has been practiced throughout history, with various specific guidelines and purposes.

Fasting is often seen as a form of self-discipline, purification, and a way to draw closer to God.

Aside from its spiritual aspects, fasting is also embraced for health reasons. Some people engage in intermittent fasting or specific dietary fasting patterns to support weight management, improve metabolic health, or enhance overall well-being.

It's important to note that while fasting can have health benefits, it should be approached with caution, and individuals with certain medical conditions or concerns should consult with a healthcare professional before beginning a fasting regimen.

Fasting has been an important part of my growth in God. I love fasting weekly even if it's just for a few hours unless the Lord didn't allow me or a medical concern.

Jesus said, "And he said unto them, This kind can come forth by nothing, but by prayer and fasting." (Mark 9:29 KJV).

I had to discipline my flesh and abstain from eating in order to draw closer to God, which ultimately strengthened me spiritually.

Fasting became something that I love and enjoy doing it. I'm not just eating and feeding my body, but I'm feeding spiritually on the word of God and when I worship during fasting time the spiritual connection to God is easier.

There is a more divine connection with God when you fast. Your spirit man now has the time for you to focus on him, the Holy Spirit and not just eating to keep your physical body. I desired healing and deliverance from the tormenting spirits that had plagued my life and fasting did it.

I recognized the importance of approaching fasting with the right mindset, ensuring that anger and unforgiveness didn't prevail within me. Fasting required a calm spirit and a prepared mind, and it was crucial to avoid strengthening negative spirits, allowing the Holy Spirit to assume control instead.

Preparing the mind, body, and spirit was essential for a fasting experience that would yield positive spiritual outcomes.

The objective of fasting was not to be possessed by demons or weakened but to undergo healing and deliverance, either during or after the fasting period.

"Is not this the fast that I have chosen? to loose the bands of wickedness, to undo the heavy burdens, and to let the oppressed go free, and that ye break every yoke?" (Isaiah 58:6 KJV)

The Lord has fasting set to bring changes and deliverance into our lives. Even Jesus had to fast after he got baptized to be strengthen for his ministry and know what his Father Jehovah wanted him to do even though he was God himself.

The devil tempted Jesus right after he finished his fasting so you will be tempted, but you can use the word of God just like Jesus to resist the devil and defeat him.

After a fast I work to keep myself calm, listen for what God has to tell me and see what has changed in my life. I feel the difference in my body, mind and spirit.

One of the greatest things about fasting is it opens up the spiritual realm to bring your blessings to you, but only if you do the fasting right as how God mentions in Isaiah 58:6:

"Is not this the fast that I have chosen? to loose the bands of wickedness, to undo the heavy burdens, and to let the oppressed go free, and that ye break every yoke?"

When you fast and seek God's intervention, He may send someone to pray for your healing, deliverance, or share a prophecy, depending on your specific requests. Sometimes, an Angel of God may visit you during this time.

In my experiences, I've encountered breathtaking scenes—a beautiful garden and celestial creatures beyond human imagination, receive deliverance and healing. In these divine moments, I received instructions on how to overcome the challenges I was struggling with.

Additionally, a crucial aspect of fasting involves meditating on the word of God throughout the fasting period. The Word is a source of life, providing the strength, vitality, and divine revelations needed for a deeper understanding of God and His plans for your life.

As Proverbs 4:20-22 (KJV) emphasizes,

"attend to my words; Incline thine ear unto my sayings. Let them not depart from thine eyes; Keep them in the midst of thine heart. For they are life unto those that find them, And health to all their flesh."

Therefore, fasting is not only a physical discipline but also a spiritual journey where God's word becomes a guiding force for strength, life, health, and profound revelations.

PROPHETIC SOUND KEMEKA

HOW I BECAME PROPHETIC SOUND KEMEKA

For I know the thoughts that I think toward you, saith the LORD, thoughts of peace, and not of evil, to give you an expected end. (Jeremiah 29:11)

Engaging in prayer and fasting has been instrumental in shaping my identity as Prophetic Sound Kemeka.

I reached out to the Lord, seeking understanding about *who I am and my purpose*. Despite my dedication to church and service, I grappled with challenges in various aspects of my life.

To find the answers I sought, I had to separate myself from people and food, entering a period of desperation for God's guidance. As Matthew 5:6 (KJV) states:

"Blessed are they which do hunger and thirst after righteousness: for they shall be filled."

In a significant dream, I found myself on a young donkey being led on a transformative journey on the road, the river side and over the bridge. Passing through diverse landscapes, including a dark valley with snakes hanging from trees, my fear was dispelled by the appearance of a man in white—Jesus Christ.

He guided me safely through the valley into a beautiful garden where people were present, marking the second profound encounter with Jesus in my life.

I believe that this was the Lord calling me back to accept my calling to becoming his Prophetess that I rejected in the past.

217

My journey involves continual growth in my spiritual gifts, and even before others recognized it, I sensed my role as a prophetess. The confirmation came when people around me began prophesying and addressing me as a prophetess, affirming what I already knew.

From my early years, I experienced moments where I heard and foresaw events before their occurrence. Prophecy naturally emerged during prayers, worship, ministry, or everyday conversations, whenever the Lord imparted a word for someone.

In response to God's call, I pledged to follow His will unconditionally, avoiding past compromises that disappointed my Father Jehovah.

Embracing this calling comes with challenges; there will be friends, family, or others who may harbor resentment or label me as overly righteous. Enduring such animosity is painful, yet I draw strength from Jesus' teaching to His disciples:

"Blessed are they which are persecuted for righteousness' sake: for theirs is the kingdom of heaven" (Matthew 5:10 KJV).

In this commitment to righteousness, I find solace and purpose, knowing that despite the challenges, I walk the path designated by my divine calling.

Years ago, the Lord revealed to me a divine purpose—to aid women, young women, men and children who endure various forms of abuse: physical, mental, verbal, sexual, and spiritual.

Little did I know that this calling would manifest in the public sphere, as I found myself ministering live on platforms like

Facebook, YouTube, TikTok, and Instagram. My husband Pastor Kelly, who is a broadcasting engineer set up my studio equipment.

The journey to this point was riddled with personal struggles, particularly my hesitancy to go live. I feared rejection and criticism, compounded by my own challenges with pronunciation.

A pivotal moment occurred when my husband, Pastor Kelly, connected me with Prophetess Light, a gospel singer and prophetess from Nigeria. During their conversation, she discerned my struggle with suicide and prayed for me.

Her encouragement ignited a newfound determination to fulfill the ministry God had called me to. Despite initial reluctance, I realized there were women eagerly awaiting support through their own struggles.

God confirmed that this was my calling by allowing women who had been hurt to ask me for advice.

Rather than merely sending texts or engaging in face-to-face interactions, the Holy Spirit guided me toward a broader form of outreach—going live on social media.

This decision marked a new level of evangelism, a platform where I could offer guidance and support to a wider audience. Each Tuesday, I faced spiritual attacks and moments of weakness, yet, through prayer and reliance on the Holy Spirit, I found the strength to persevere.

When the Lord prompted me to go live on Thursday, I responded, "Lord, I am weary from work, and it has been a while."

Later, while attending church services in 2023, I heard the Holy Spirit said to have Sunday services, and I wondered how that could be feasible. However, I remembered that He is the God of possibilities, and so I began conducting three services a week through the guidance of the Holy Spirit.

I received confirmation from the Holy Spirit on more than two occasions regarding these services, supported by individuals who believed in my ministry.

The scripture from Zechariah 4:6 became a guiding force:

"Not by might, nor by power, but by my spirit, saith the Lord of hosts,"

It emphasized the divine source of strength and resilience, reinforcing the understanding that this ministry wasn't about my capabilities alone but a partnership with the Spirit of the Lord.

As I confronted and conquered my fears and uncertainties, I discerned the transformative potential of embracing God's calling in the vast realm of social media. It became a potent avenue for evangelism, outreach, and ministering to those struggling with various challenges.

The digital platform allowed me to extend the reach of my ministry, connecting with individuals in need on a broader scale.

The realization of my ministry's impact on social media

underscored that the strength and resilience I experienced were not solely attributable to my capabilities. Instead, it highlighted a profound partnership with the Spirit of the Lord.

The source of power wasn't grounded in my own might or skills but was, indeed, a divine collaboration.

In my commitment to God, I made vows and pledged to honor them. During a quiet moment on my altar, a divine revelation unfolded. It was quiet and I heard '***Prophetic Sound***.'

I said Prophetic Sound, that's the name of the ministry and my name is ***Prophetic Sound Kemeka***.

I asked what my company name will be and I heard ***Prophetic Sound Empire***. I didn't choose the name the Lord gave to me, but I will use it until He comes to take me home.

"For many are called, but few are chosen." Matthew 22:14 KJV.

In a dream, I encountered a homeless man and moved by compassion, I provided him the safety of my sofa for him to sleep on. However, the situation took an unexpected turn when the man expressed inappropriate intentions, seeking intimacy with me.

Resolute in my commitment to serving Jesus Christ, I firmly declined his advances, asserting my dedication to a higher purpose.

Despite the man's physical attractiveness, I maintained my conviction and refused to compromise my principles. His subsequent attempt to exert influence by summoning flies as a form of attack was met with unwavering faith.

Through the powerful name of Jesus Christ, I overcame the adversity posed by these symbolic pests, affirming my allegiance to my Lord and Savior.

This dream serves as a testament to my unwavering commitment to serving Jesus Christ and upholding moral integrity. The rejection of worldly temptations and the victorious triumph over symbolic challenges underscore my dedication to a life guided by faith and divine principles.

My initial encounter happened while I was atop a building, surrounded by demons. I distinctly heard a voice proclaiming, "I will never forget this."

Suddenly, a man appeared before me, adorned in sandals and a flowing white robe, though his face remained unseen. He beckoned me to follow him, and with each step he took, I mirrored his movement precisely.

As demons approached, striking at me, I found myself shielded, not allowing me to be harmed.

Since that moment, I've been faithfully following in the footsteps of Jesus Christ, finding protection from both demons and adversaries.

In 2015; I begin thinking about what a visiting Pastor from Antigua confirmed that the Lord intended to utilize everything I had experienced.

Although unsure of how this would unfold, I simply desired God's love, regardless of the shame from my past. Prophetess

Fire later prophesied that I would become a General for God and ascend to the third heavens, leaving me to wonder about the specifics of God's plan.

He began preparing me during my first ministry school in 2012, where I became a licensed Evangelist. Although instructed by the Elder not to use the title when he was the one that said I was an Evangelist, I adhered until it was confirmed by God through Prophetess Light and Pastor Fortune from Nigeria, who affirmed that I was ordained by God as an Evangelist.

Subsequently, during my second ministry school in 2014, I obtained an Associate's in Theology.

In 2020, I discovered Destiny Training Academy led by Dr. Faith Wokoma. I enrolled in her mentorship program focused on inner healing to address my internal wounds.

Additionally, I participated in other courses offered, including Healing and Deliverance, as I frequently experienced dreams of praying for people's healing and deliverance.

I watched various leaders who taught sound doctrine of God to learn about God and during some of those services, God spoke through the leaders, and I learned what it was the Lord required of me.

Right now, He was requiring that I use my voice and God-given gifts to spread the Good News on social media. He also required of me to share my testimony through the writing of this book. Prophetess Natalie Smith told me few years ago that the Lord wants me to write a book about what I have been through and now I did it.

I was given the mantle of a Prophet by Prophet Dabson then Prophetess Light, Pastor Roger called me Evangelist then not long after a Prophetess, Pastor Errol White called me Prophetess and other Men and Women of God.

A year later, Apostle Shepherd laid her hands upon me releasing the mantle of Prophet and Evangelist.

In 2023, during a prophetic encounter, the male Prophet informed my mother that I had been filled with the Holy Spirit from her womb.

Surprised, I sought confirmation from God.

He provided the answer through a Pastor's teachings on YouTube, explaining how a baby can be filled with the Holy Spirit from the womb when the mother is fill with Holy Spirit.

Additionally, during a service 'TheGospel' hosted by my husband Pastor Kelly and myself; the Lord reminded me of

past encounters during my teenage years, where His power overwhelmed me, leading me to dance in the spirit.

Through these experiences, God confirmed that I had indeed been filled with the Holy Spirit, from my mother's womb.

One night, the Lord revealed to me a vision of holding a book in my hand, as I flipped through its pages, I witnessed videos of my life—it was my book of life.

In December 2023, I experienced a vision of myself walking and extending my hands, as a man reached out, took my hands, and walked alongside me.

Though I couldn't see his face, I recognized him as the same person who had previously instructed me to follow him, who was Jesus Christ.

During prayer, the Lord impressed upon me Jeremiah 1:4-5

"Then the word of the Lord came unto me, saying, Before I formed thee in the belly I knew thee; and before thou camest forth out of the womb I sanctified thee, and I ordained thee a prophet unto the nations."

and Mark 16:15-18 (NIV):

He said to them, "Go into all the world and preach the gospel to all creation. Whoever believes and is baptized will be saved, but whoever does not believe will be condemned. And these signs will accompany those who believe: In my name they will drive out demons; they will speak in new tongues; they will pick up snakes with their hands; and when they drink deadly poison, it will not hurt them at all; they will place their hands on sick people, and they will get well."

In declaring my identity as PropheticSoundKemeka La Toya Benjamin-Williams, I embrace a profound calling— a mother to many nations, a Global Mother, and God's Solution to many. Bringing healing and deliverance to people through the Holy Spirit.

This self-identification signifies a purpose-driven existence, reflecting my role as a nurturing force with a global impact.

Through this declaration, I align myself with a divine mission, seeking to bring solutions and spiritual guidance to those entrusted to my care.

I am PropheticSoundKemeka La Toya Benjamin-Williams- a mother to the many nations- Global Mother- God's Solution to many. Bringing healing and deliverance to people through the Holy Spirit.

DICTIONARY

<u>Molestation</u>
n. the crime of sexual acts with children up to the age of 18, including touching of private parts, exposure of genitalia, taking of pornographic pictures, rape, inducement of sexual acts with the molester or with other children and variations of these acts by pedophiles. Molestation also applies to incest by a relative with a minor family member and any unwanted sexual acts with adults short of rape.

https://dictionary.law.com/Default.aspx?selected=1274

<u>Incest</u>
To <u>engage</u> in sexual <u>activities</u> with one who is of blood <u>relations</u>.
https://www.urbandictionary.com/define.php?term=Incest

<u>Masturbation</u> is the sexual stimulation of one's own genitals for sexual arousal or other sexual pleasure, usually to the point of orgasm.[1][2][3] The stimulation may involve hands, fingers, everyday objects, sex toys such as vibrators, or combinations of these.[1][2] Manual sex is masturbation with a sexual partner,[3][4] and may include manual stimulation of a partner's genitals (fingering or a hand job),[4] or be used as a form of non-penetrative sex.[5]
https://en.m.wikipedia.org/wiki/Masturbation

Homosexuality is romantic attraction, sexual attraction, or sexual behavior between members of the same sex or gender.[1][2][3] As a sexual orientation, homosexuality is "an enduring pattern of emotional, romantic, and/or sexual attractions" to people of the same sex. It "also refers to a person's sense of identity based on those attractions, related behave

iors, and membership in a community of others who share those attractions."[4][5]

https://en.m.wikipedia.org/wiki/Homosexuality

Pornography (colloquially known as **porn** or **porno**) has been defined as sexual subject material "such as a picture, video, or text," that is considered sexually arousing.[a] Indicated for the consumption by adults, pornography depictions have evolved from cave paintings, some forty millennia ago, to virtual reality presentations in modern-day. Pornography use is considered a widespread recreational activity among people in-line with other digitally mediated activities such as use of social media or video games. [b] A distinction is often made regarding adult content as whether to classify it as pornography or erotica.

Lust intense sexual desire or appetite.

https://www.dictionary.com/browse/lust

REFERENCES

"None of you shall approach any one of his close relatives to uncover nakedness. I am the Lord."
Leviticus 18:6 ESV
https://bible.com/bible/59/lev.18.6.ESV

Psalms 5:12: *"For thou, Lord, wilt bless the righteous; with favour wilt thou compass him as with a shield.*" **(pg 17)**
King James Bible. Published...   Author....

John 3:36: *"If the Son therefore shall make you free, ye shall be free indeed."* **(pg20)**

Exodus 20:13: *"Thou shalt not kill."* **(pg 29)**

Luke 6:37: *"forgive, and ye shall be forgiven"* **(pg 31)**

Romans 12:19: *"Dearly beloved, avenge not yourselves, but rather   give   place   unto   wrath: for it **is** written, **Vengeance is mine**; I will repay, saith the Lord."*
Pg 37

Ephesians 5:18: *"And be not drunk with wine, wherein is excess; but be filled with the Spirit".* **Pg 38**

Genesis 19:32: *"Come, let us make our father drink wine, and we will lie with him, that we may preserve seed of our father.*" **PG 38**

1 Samuel 1:14-15: *"And Eli said unto her, How long wilt thou be drunken?"* **PG 39**

Mark 14:22-24: *"And as they did eat, Jesus took bread, and blessed, and brake it, and gave to them, and said, Take, eat: this is my body. And he took the cup, and when he had given thanks, he gave it to them: and they all drank of it. And he said unto them, This is my blood of the new testament, which is shed for many."* **PG 39**

1 Timothy 5:23: *"Stop drinking only water, and use a little wine because of your stomach and your frequent illnesses."* (NIV). **PG 39**

Genesis 3:16: *"Unto the woman he said. And thy desire shall be to thy husband, and he shall rule over thee".* **Pg 45**

Romans 1:27-28: *"And likewise also the men, leaving the natural use of the woman, burned in their lust one toward another; men with men working that which is unseemly, and receiving in themselves that recompence of their error which was meet. And even as they did not like to retain God in their knowledge, God gave them over to a reprobate mind, to do those things which are not convenient."* pg 46-47

1 John 2:16: *"For all that is in the world, the lust of the flesh, and the lust of the eyes, and the pride of life, is not of the Father, but is of the world."* **PG 61**

Mark 11:26: *"But if ye do not forgive, neither will your Father which is in heaven forgive your trespasses"* PG 74

Matthew 10:16: *"Behold, I send you forth as sheep in the midst of wolves: be ye therefore wise as serpents, and harmless as doves".* **Pg 75**

Luke 8:2: *"And certain women, which had been healed of evil spirits and infirmities, Mary called Magdalene, out of whom went seven devils,"* PG 75

James 4:7: *"Be strong and of a good courage, fear not, nor be afraid of them: for the LORD thy God, he it is that doth go with thee; he will not fail thee, nor forsake thee."*

Deuteronomy 31:6 KJV: *"Is not this the fast that I have chosen? to loose the bands of wickedness, to undo the heavy burdens, and to let the oppressed go free, and that ye break every yoke?"*

Romans 8:26-27 KJV: *"Likewise the Spirit also helpeth our infirmities: for we know not what we should pray for as we ought: but the Spirit itself maketh intercession for us with groanings which cannot be uttered."*

Matthew 6:13 KJV: "And lead us not into temptation, but deliver us from evil: For thine is the kingdom, and the power, and the glory, forever. Amen."

Genesis 1:26 ESV: *"Then God said, "Let us make man in our image, after our likeness. And let them have dominion over the fish of the sea and over the birds of the heavens and over the* livestock and over all the earth and over every creeping thing that creeps on the earth."

Romans 12:19 KJV: " *Dearly beloved, avenge not yourselves, but rather give place unto wrath: for it is written, Vengeance is mine; I will repay, saith the Lord.* "

Deuteronomy 32:30 KJV: "*How should one chase a thousand, And two put ten thousand to flight, Except their Rock had sold them, And the LORD had shut them up?* "

Matthew 5:44 KJV: "*But I say unto you, Love your enemies, bless them that curse you, do good to them that hate you, and pray for them which despitefully use you, and persecute you.* "

1 Corinthians 12:10 KJV: "*To another the working of miracles; to another prophecy; to another discerning of spirits; to another divers kinds of tongues; to another the interpretation of tongues.* "

1 Corinthians 14:15 KJV: "*What is it then? I will pray with the spirit, and I will pray with the understanding also: I will sing with the spirit, and I will sing with the understanding also.* "

Mark 9:29 KJV: "*And he said unto them, This kind can come forth by nothing, but by prayer and fasting.* "

Proverbs 4:20-22 KJV: "*My son, attend to my words; Incline thine ear unto my sayings. Let them not depart from thine eyes;*

Keep them in the midst of thine heart. For they are life unto those that find them, And health to all their flesh."

Matthew 5:6 KJV: "*Blessed are they which do hunger and thirst after righteousness: for they shall be filled.*"

Matthew 5:10 JV: "*Blessed are they which are persecuted for righteousness' sake: for theirs is the kingdom of heaven.*"